Spice

"Viewing Life through a Grown Woman's Perspective"

By

Crystal Pringle & V. Darrell Lloyd
With
Geneva Baker Cotton

Spice- See Issues

Copyright © 2015

Crystal Pringle and V. Darrell Lloyd

All rights reserved

PUBLISHED BY
Grown Woman Productions.

Dedication

To Geneva Baker Cotton and Vivian Reed…the
original Spice –See Women from whom this concept
emerges

Table of Contents

Acknowledgements

I have grown so much in the process of writing this work. In order to get the most for these dialogues I had to listen to a number of conversations from a number of ladies addressing numerous issues. I never knew how much I had to learn and even the things I had learned needed to be seen through a different set of eyes.

I thank so many of you for allowing me to look through your eyes and from your points of view to understand very sensitive issues. Special thanks go to my co-writer and consultant Crystal for your love and an ear that can hear and translate what I cannot. I also thank our collaborative partner and continuing infuser of thought Geneva Baker-Cotton for keeping things fresh and flowing. You encouragement to see things through excellently has been monumental. I also would like to thank Kim Ricks, Wendy Cason, Carolyn Foster, Eva Beck, Donna McMiller, Tanisha Johnson, Belinda Williams and Jonessa Williams for an abundance of insight. Tracy-Pringle McBride and Renee Pringle have been that REAL source of truth, example and laughter and a strong presence in the spirit of this work. I also thank my daughters Ashlee and Amber for bringing their dad from the finishing line of adolescence into their new vista as women.

I thank those of you including my friends Dedra Nelson, Patricia Stephens, Belinda Bell and Bernice Nelson for your support and true friendship To those of you I did not call this time that know that you are special to me I say "Thank You."

God bless you in all things.

Introduction

It is possible to see something while standing with a person and get a totally different perspective than they did. It is possible to walk away from the same place and debate what was actually seen. How? Change places. Change angles. Change shoes. Your view is dependent upon where you stand.

Spice-See Dialogues is the recording of a man, named Seer, who is invited into the presence of a number of women and taught to see things from their perspective. He is amazed and educated because he is a man. His view or perspective is from a different point of view. He was missing things that made him less capable of deeper understanding and communication.

The group of ladies in SPICEE are from a diverse number of backgrounds including corporate financial backgrounds, health care backgrounds, faith backgrounds, educational backgrounds, domestic and a variety of ethnic and social groups.

You will find things you agree with and things that may make you uncomfortable. You will find things that may seem controversial and challenge you. The goal in these dialogues is not to determine who is right or wrong but creating a dialogue that enables us to communicate and work through issues by becoming sensitive and committed to each other. These are great for your church or community reading group. Your Life will be changed and challenged.
S.P.I.C.E.E.

Sisters
Participating
In
Conversation
Empowering
Each Other

How to Enjoy this Book

Before you get started let me give you a few basic instructions for reading this book. It is for your enjoyment. It is for your inspiration. It is for education. Each story is written in a narrative poetic style. It is designed to be easily read and draw you into an actual experience. The experiences are of women from varying backgrounds and presented for the group to engage in well thought out consideration and dialogue.

Some situations will be easier to identify with and others will provide some deeper complexities. I take no position in these pieces but present them for you to work through them and get the maximum benefit. These pieces may be presented topically, dramatically or in whatever other manner that you choose.

Each situation piece concludes with two sheets at the end of it. One is entitled "On the Table" and leads the reader into dialogue on what the perceived issues are in it. Participants are led to interact with each other and put these issues on the table so that they can definitively deal with them. Sheet two is entitled "Out the Door" and is designed to lead the participant into consideration of how she can address the issue after the discussion is over and after and considerations are made. The discussion allows the participant to also learn the various responses of others that may differ from theirs and begin to respectfully interact with them.

This is a book about acceptance and understanding. It is for the purpose of thinking, dealing with, engaging and accepting each other where we are, for who we are and what God is doing in us while we become. Remember to share…This is not for argument but for understanding and communication.

Enjoy your time with God. Enjoy the time with each other. Welcome to Spice~See Conversations.

"It all began with a Taxi Ride….."

Vee: It is a beautiful day and I plan to enjoy it. I need to get a little religion in here after last night.

Eva: Last night? What did we do so wrong last night?

Vee: We? You are innocent but I cannot tell you some things that went on in my mind. Did I call you innocent? No...You just have not been exposed. Come on and let's get ready to go.

Eva: You are the bad girl. I am no way as bad as you are so quit playing.

Vee: Meet me at the altar in a few hours and let the Lord decide. The one left as the pile of ashes following the AMEN is the guiltiest one.

Eva: Deal! Who is picking us up?

Vee: Pastor said he will identify himself at the door.

Eva: I wonder if he is cute.

Vee: Cute? He needs to be fine. I don't have time for cute no more. Fine is the order of the day. It is too long of a ride to be surrounded by chauffeur ugliness.

Eva: See...I told you that you are bad.

Vee: Come on in the kitchen and quit that foolishness you are talking. Pastor has some pies in here and I am going to take a piece just in case I get a little lunchy before they feed us.

Eva: Yes, I am Catholic by profession and one thing we know how to do is make it through a service with the meal not yet completely digested. Those Baptist and Pentecostal folks with let the meal digest and take t=you through a half day fast before the service is over.

Vee: This is a Pentecostal church isn't it?

Eva: Oh Yes....

Vee: I better get two pieces then.

Eva: Cut me two also...Hey, is that the doorbell?

Vee: Yes it is.

Eva: Let me get it. (Opening door) Come on in. Are you here to pick us up?

Ike: Pick you up? Who are you? I came to pick up some pies to take to the church for the Pastor.

Eva: Vee call the police

Vee: What?

Eva: Call the police. This man is trying to rob the kitchen and take these pies.

Vee: Hit him then. I am coming.

Ike: Wait...Wait...

Eva: Why would pastor have you come to get all these pies?

Vee: Aren't you here to pick us up?

Ike: I thought that I....

Eva;   You have the right to remain silent

Vee: Or we can silence you with a few of these utensils for trying to steal these pies.

Ike: You can ask Pastor...

Eva: Uh huh... You know he is sleep

Vee; Are you heading to the church?

Ike: Yes...

Eva: Good! We need a ride. Are you a good driver?

Ike: Very good and very safe.

Ike: Since that last accident I had in 1984 I have been very safe. I lost my left eye when that drunk driver hit me.

Eva: Did you get a new one?

Vee: How are you going to get a new eye Eva? That is a silly question.

Eva: Is your windshield clean? Wait! It is raining and cloudy...Are you sure we should ride with you?

Ike: I am most efficient. After we get the pies...

Eva: Back up buddy. There will be no pie heist here.

Ike: Call the pastor.

Vee: Let's go sir. We can do the pie thing later.

Ike: On the way I have a book I would like for you to read.

Eva: We will read it later.

Ike: I would appreciate your opinion.

Vee: Later...

Ike: My niece is a very good writer

Eva: Listen pie burglar...we are heading to a conference. We will get with the book later.

Ike: Let us go.

         (In the car)

Ike: We are ready

Eva: Keep your eyes on the road and get us there safe.

Vee: Stop being funny

Eva: What?

Vee: He only has that one eye.

Eva: Oh!

Vee: Ike which one of your eyes is gone:

Ike: The right one but I drive (turning around)

Eva: Get you eye on the road!

Ike: I am fine

Eva: Keep your eye on the road.

Vee: Yes, it is raining, the windshield is dirty and you are turning around with the good eye and letting the gone eye look out for us. Keep your eyes on the road.

Ike: I have not had an accident

Eva: Because that good eye is functioning. Drive and keep your eye on the road.

Vee: We are going to need a real good dose of religion today.

Eva: You are going to need an overdose.

Vee: Why...?
Ike: (Turning around again) you ladies are most funny and...

Both: DRIVE!!

Ike: I am a good multi-tasker.

Eva: Well we are trying to avoid a multi-car accident with multiple injuries because you do not have multiple eyes and are looking the wrong way with the singular one.

Vee: Keep your eyes...oops...eye on the road.

Eva: We do not want his eye on the road. If that happens then he will have none in his head and this ride will be sure dangerous.

Vee: Stop! You need to behave!

Ike: (Turning around again) you ladies are most beautiful and....

Vee: Ike!!!! Keep your eyes upfront!

Ike: My niece's book is...

Eva: We will read the book but you need to get us to church on time.

Vee: Yes, didn't the church used to be a famous club?

Eva: Yes, but the Lord has done a marvelous work on it. It is a place of awesome people in the Lord now.

Vee: I don't think that you are saved like you ought to be Eva.

Eva: (Laughing) Listen to you! I am a good girl.

Vee: So you think…Sneaking a drink last night when you did not think anyone was looking…

Eva: I did that openly and gave you some too…

Vee: Oh yeah!

Eva: AND….you drank it!

Ike: I like to take a casual drink now and then

Vee: Did you have one last night.

Eva: Oh No! Cloudy day, raining, dirty windshield, one eye and driving under the influence….

Vee: Stop it girl!

Eva: If the Lord does not help us…

Ike: We are almost at the church

Vee: Uh, let's see. Ike you want this pie back here?

Ike: Most certainly.

Vee: Let's make a deal…

Ike: What is the deal?

Vee: Take us to the Blue Note Jazz Club

Eva: What? I thought we were going to the church.

Vee: Well, we did kind of sort of go…

Eva: When?

Ike: Drive by the church. Do not stop but just drive by it.

Eva: What did that prove?

Vee: We went by the church. We did not stop but we did go by. You do not have to share all the details with everybody. They have no business being so nosey anyway.

Vee: Ike you cannot tell pastor

Ike: What shall I tell him when he asks what happened to you?

Vee: Tell him that you took us by the church and after we got out the car you did not see us.

Eva: Tell him we got out the car on the side where your lost eye is.

Ike: You girls are too much…

Vee: Ike?

Ike: Yes Mam….

Vee: Remember that you know nothing

Ike: Will you read my niece's book?

Vee: Yes…pick us up after the sessions are over so we can go to lunch.

Eva: We want to get there for the offering so there will be no suspicion as to where we have been.

Vee: We will have to use one of these little beige lies I have.

Eva: Beige?

Vee: Yes… It's been used a little and is not quite white any more.

Eva: Put on your shades girl.

Vee: Oh yeah…

Eva: (Exiting vehicle) The Lord knows we are not supposed to be here but…let's go!

Vee: It will be fun!
Eva: Lord this is Vee's fault.

Vee: Are you talking about me?

Eva: Just to the Lord…Come on girl

Vee: Let's get a table…do you think anyone else from church here?

Eva: Not yet! They may be coming but remember that they are Pentecostal-Baptist. They will not be here for a lonnnnng time.

Vee: Oh yes….

Eva: Let's take some…

Vee: Don't you say it. I know you are catholic but there is no communion wine in here.

Eva: Come on girl. Just pull up a chair. Let's have them pour us a drink and let's talk a while.

Vee: That is good with me…

Eva: I thought the driver was going to be cute

Vee: I told you we needed fine…not cute but fine.

Eva: Oh Yeah ~

…And then it continued at a club

Vee: It is cool in here

Eva: You know we are going to hell don't you?

Vee: Why?

Eva: Skipping church?

Vee: Nobody knows where we are?

Eva: The Lord knows…

Vee…And the driver

Eva: The pie will take care of him

Vee: Yep!

Eva: What?

Vee: We going to hell

Eva: Well we may as well enjoy the journey

Vee: Is that Sis. Reynolds there?

Eva: You know better

Vee: Why do you say that?

Eva: You know she is Baptist!

Vee: Yes, but I am sure that is her and look at that dress she has on!

Eva: Oh my…I can see her navel and she is not raising her dress!

Ray: Excuse me ladies

Vee: No need for excuse. How are you Mr. Fine Man?

Ray: Are you flirting me?

Vee: No! I am just stating a fact. Do not make too much of it. How many eyes do you have?

Eva: What?

Ray: I do not understand…

Vee: Do you have two good eyes? Why do you wear glasses? Can you really see? Do you own a German Shepherd with a harness? Is that a fraternity cane or something else…? Ray?

Ray: I am out….

Vee: Bye Sweetheart

Eva: What did you do? Why did you do that?

Vee: Kill it before it grows. I have seen that act before. I was not interested in scene II

Eva: We going to hell

Vee: Right! Is that Kay?

Eva: Yes… Hey Kay

Kay: Hey! What are the two of you doing here? That does not look like grape juice in that cup.

Vee: No but it is made with WHOLLY (with a "w") water and Scotch.

Eva: We going to Hell…

Kay: Eva why are you all here?

Eva: That dang taxi driver we had got lost and dropped us off at the club.

Vee: We came in here for a coke to refresh ourselves before we went back to the women's conference and then decided to rest our feet and do a little evangelism for the people in here are in a dark place and if you believe that you are well…you are going to hell just like Eva.

Kay: I am here because I need a break from people.

Eva: So what are you calling us?

Kay: I mean…

Vee: Do not mind Eva…she still is rattled by that cab driver from this morning…

Kay: What…

Eva: So what is wrong with you? Come in and sit.

Vee: Isn't that Tina?

Eva: What? She should be at work…at the church

Kay: She is a Christian?

Eva: Yes

Kay: She is a regular here.

Vee: How do you know?

Kay: I am too…I come here to relax and unwind plus there is a one eyed fellow that comes in here all the time and offers to buy me a drink if I will read his niece's book.

Eva: Oh my Gosh....

Vee: That...

Eva: He is going to hell too
Tina: Ladies are in the house

Eva: Why aren't you at church?

Tina: Looks like the Conference is here

Eva: Why aren't you at church?

Tina: Man problems...

Vee: Oh...you need to talk?

Tina: Yes, but to that fine man over there

Eva: Get back over here

Tina: But I have needs...

Eva: Girl hush. You are angry and horny and he is a quick fix with long term consequences. Keep your panties on and water down your hormones.

Tina: He is coming over here

Vee: Oh my Eva he is gorgeous

Tina: Let me go for just a moment...

Vee: Sit down and have a drink girl. Let me handle this.

Tim: Hello ladies

Vee: Hello handsome. I know that you came over here to go fishing and my girl Tina here loves your bait and will gladly let your fine self hook her but we are the "Aint no booty here to be gotten committee of the local Baptist-Pentecostal Church" and you look like heaven but a girl will go through hell messing with you so step on before somebody gets hurt or addictively pleasured and the Lord comes back and you wind up in hell…

Tim: So…

Eva: You are booty hunting and we are trying to keep a sister out the trap…although she may be hunting too.

Tina: Here is my number…

Vee: She is the church secretary

Tim: What?

Eva: Yep!

Kay: She should…

Vee: Hush girl…Tim?

Tim: Step on Baby…you are fine a hell but well…aint nobody got time for it.

Eva: Dismissed!

Tim: Okay…

Tina: I do not believe what you all just did

Eva: Didn't you say you were having man problems?

Tina: Yes, but I …

Vee: Would have had one more

Eva: That looks like Mary

Vee: That is my girl. Let me holler at her
        Hey Mary....

Mary: Vee? What are you doing here?

Vee: Just doing a little evangelistic work and you know...
Mary: I understand girl.

Vee: So what's up?

Mary: Where shall I start?

Eva: Pull up a chair.

Vee: I thought we were going to the conference.

Eva: The conference is here. What's your problem Mary?

Mary: Children! I am tired of doing the single mother thing and need
        these ungrateful folks out my house.

Vee: Put them out

Eva: Put them out now!

Tina: Put them way out...

Kay: Whoop some....

Vee: Don't set her off just yet

Eva: When was the last time you got some...?

Tina: Got some what?

Eva: You know what I am talking about

Tina: Oh… well…

Tim: I can share if you have needs…

Vee: Take your nasty fine behind self on…

Eva: Yes, remember that we are from the LABATCAWWRIL.

Tim: What is that?
Eva: Local Anti-Booty at the Club Association of Women Who Will Regret it Later.

Vee: Our motto is "If it does not belong to you it should not be up in you."

Eva: Let the church say AMEN!

Tim: All of you are saved?

Vee: No!

Eva: Some of us are going to hell…

Tim: What?

Vee: See you later hunter

Tim: My name is Tim.

Vee: Yes, but you are definitely hunting so take all that fine maleness away from this brood of hungering ladies who will turn you out if you keep standing her looking all delicious despite your obvious shallowness.

Tina: I think…

Eva: Come on ladies…let's go to church

Kay: Church?

Eva: Yes… church?

Tina: Why:

Eva: You know you have to go.

Tina: Why?

Eva: So you can mark us present in attendance and no one will know where we have been. Besides I need to be there for the free lunch.

Vee: How do we call the driver?

Eva: He is right over there at the bar

Vee: What?

Kay: The fellow with the Book…that is him

Vee: And what is he doing to that woman?

Eva: He is offering her potato pie….let's go. Ladies let us go to the conference and then if you want we can meet up somewhere and continue this conversation.

Kay: Yes, I need to talk bad.

Tina: I need to talk to that man…

Eva: Come back over here with your nasty self.

Vee: After church and lunch…bring a friend.

Eva: We will be looking for you. You need not be coy or fearful. You can be real. Don't bring your man, children or anyone that causes you to be any less than who you are or what you REALLY are feeling. When you enter the place just come in. The door will be open to you. Refreshments will be available so just pour yourself a drink and prepare to sit a while. Let's just have some Grown Woman Conversation.

Vee: You may be living heaven or going through hell but let's just talk.

Eva: Let's get to church and we may not have to go to hell.

Vee: Driver! Bring me a piece of that pie and take us to church
Eva: And you better believe that we are going to tell pastor that you brought us to the club if you breathe a word of this.

Ike: But I....

All: Drive!!!!!!!

Eva: Make sure you keep the good eye on the road

TO BE CONTINUED...

NOW IT IS BEFORE YOU! WHAT ARE YOUR ISSUES? WHAT IS ON YOUR MIND? TURN THE PAGES. GROWN WOMEN ARE PUTTING THINGS ON THE TABLE. THEY ARE FINDING WHAT THEY CAN TAKE OUT THE DOOR!

Spice-See Issues

"Viewing Life from a Grown Woman's Perspective"

FROM A GROWN WOMAN
TO A YOUNG LADY

Sit down baby and talk to me
Welcome to womanhood
Oh~ I know you've got the goods
The curves and parts that take the eyes
The legs, the breasts, the butt and thighs
And that's all good but you need to see
The new place you have among ladies
You are legal and on your way
To being a Grown lady one day BUT
Not quite yet

You see you have entered a new door
You are expected to know and to be more
You are fair game to many others on the field
Be careful of where you stop and to whom you yield
Learn before you leap and know before you go
Young lady be certain and take it slow
Talk to your mother and get some advice
She may not be all your flavor but you will get good spice

You may think this is not needed
But growness does not just happen it must be seeded
And womanhood from childhood/adolescence is a transition
You must work yourself into this new position
Hear me while hearing can be best communicated
Do not despise it not consider it over rated
For all you are and shall come to be
I have established and you shall inherit from me

Find your mentors and learn some valuable lessons
It will keep you from foolishness and distressing
If all of your advice comes from those your age
You will make many mistakes upon this page...
Of life and so many times you will try to erase
Things that never should have held this space

Keep your friends and circle; you need them too
But to be successful you will need history before you

You cannot be grown on your mother's dime
So before you demand sole independence keep this in mind
She can help you get what she has if you listen well
Do not lose her support coming under a spell
Of "doing your own thing because I am me"
Your mother is a grown woman and you will see
That when you go there she goes there too
And say woman to woman do what you have to do

Get and education in class and in the way
Learn your lessons and let the wisdom stay
Train to become great and make a difference
Do not let these beginning lady days be ill spent
Enjoy the learning and consider it worth the time
Living and learning are like rhythm and rhyme
Get it all while it offers you unattached
Become who you will be and you can find the right match

See yourself from the inside out
Here well what I am talking about
Develop in the inner places and you can reveal
The person you are as authentic and so real
Other women can see you and appreciate you
Because your womanhood will be through and through
Not fake and pretentious for true women can see
When you are really who you claim to be

Develop your intellect, charm and true beauty
You are more than breasts, legs and booty
And if that is what you accentuate and often share
You will only be looked upon primarily there
You shall be a piece to be had but not to be cherished
After encounters you will see men and be embarrassed
You will be like a playground open all day
Where men love to come but only to play

Keep your legs closed to visitors and strangers around
Who will see you like lost money on the ground
The will claim you and spend you until you are gone
Then whistle, walk away and with you be done
Fund no brother by giving what you have been given
You are not responsible for his living
Work side by side in together in the field
Of growth and eventually there will be a yield

Pay your own bills and care for your own self
Keep all your valuables on a special self
Do not pimp yourself for a happy meal and done nails
Your cable bill paid and some exciting tail
You run yourself
You are in charge of you
Wait on some things
It is okay to do

Learn to be by yourself
Love yourself real good
Treat yourself in the manner
You desire that another would
Teach the world who you are
Teach it how to come face to face
And engage a woman like you
Full of beauty and grace

Build a good man
By being a good lady
Manhood not maleness
Sunshine not his shady
He need not be yours
But still make an impact
By doing with lady thing well
Living on your own track

And when you find the right one
Or should I say when he finds you
Make sure that not only to him

But also to yourself you are true
Give him who you are inside first and then
If he desires to love and know that person begin
To share your true self and see where it goes
Getting to know each other is a series of flows

Marry not for money, houses, fame or sex
If you do both you and he will soon holler "NEXT"
Marry for love and who you are and can be
Are you grasping this wisdom coming from me?
Stay in your lane and strengthen your hand
Be compromising but have an equal hand
Keep your home solid; keep mess out your house
Take care of your man first ~ he is YOUR SPOUSE
Keep folks out your business
Particularly your girls
Give them that special place
But this is your world
Keep your business out the street
And when others come to look
Do not let it be found live and in print
On Twitter, Instagram and Facebook

Get your stuff together
Keep your stuff tight
Own your dignity
Do what is right…
For you and keep taking strides
Of honor with loyalty and pride
Raise the standard and the banner too
Of what womanhood is as you do what you do

Trust a sister here and a sister there
Cut the negativity about mistrusting us and share
That thought all are not perfect and some are not good
We are ever evolving together in womanhood
Walk with me daughter and this I will teach
More than what I have shared in this speech
Slow down and do not seek what I have attained

It took me many years for all of this to gain

Let me share your dreams and help you grow
Let me help you go where you desire to go
Do not forget I have been where you are going
And you can excel if you pay attention to what I am showing
Watch where I stumbled and where I have fallen
And avoid those places when defeat comes calling
I am offering these things especially for you
So that you can better do what you need to do

Live with flavor
Live with SPICE
Be sanctified naughty
With the right one but nice
Be unique
Be divine
Do who you are
Do not seek to be mine

Live young lady like a champion
Live until the first stages of lady are done
Then you can emerge on your very own
As a woman mature and fully grown
It is not about age but wisdom and experience
It is about knowledge and plain good sense
I am proud to look at you and see
The continuance of a grown woman legacy

So let's rock it now and as we take our place
You and I are different sides of the face
Of a womanhood God ordained to His glory
We are vital pages in the womanhood story
Step up now and I will step further down the line
I shall prophesy you and you shall greater define
Who we are and what we do
Grow young lady until full grown...It is what you must do!

On the Table

List the Three Major Issues that you can draw from this piece for consideration and why you consider it an issues:

1.

_____
_____
_____
_____
_____
_____
_____
_____

2.

_____
_____
_____
_____
_____
_____
_____
_____

3.

_____
_____
_____
_____
_____
_____
_____
_____

Out the Door

List what you have learned and how you can communicate and implement it better on life.

1.

_____

_____

_____

_____

_____

_____

_____

2.

_____

_____

_____

_____

_____

_____

_____

3.

_____

_____

_____

_____

_____

_____

_____

I AM SO FINE

I was standing here looking at myself
And I said to me…
You are so fine!
That's right
I spoke my mind
I look in front
Then behind
My assessment was the same
So I said it again
I am so fine~

He said I was ugly
She said she agreed
I said keep it to yourself
This I do not need
For who I am is who I see
And no other can define me
I am who I am in my mind
That is beautiful and oh so fine

Now some would be troubled at my declaration
And feel it should let another tell
Me about me but I can better see
Who I am inside of my shell
I am fine on the outside
I declare it because I know
I take care of all that I desire to show
And my fineness is not predicated on opinion
It is the assessment of the ONE
Who authenticated me…

And it was He who said I was good
Releasing me insisting I be understood
Not merely in flesh and by man

By as what He crafted me to be by His hand
And because He is still working on this masterpiece
I shall not disrespect Him nor shall I cease
To declare and write who I am upon the line
I am sweetly sufficient ~ I am fine

My opinion dictates my walk and sway
It determines where I go and where I stay
Who I share with and who I shun
Who I remain with and with whom I am done
Now do not get me wrong this is not arrogance
It is simply a fine woman's stance
You have yours and I have mine
That is part of what it means to be fine

Fineness is in my very bones
Fineness is in my presentations shown
Fineness is in my hair and eyes
Fineness is evident whether I fall or rise
Fineness knows me as a very close friend
My fineness reaches both women and men
Who can validate and will also co-sign
The declaration that states "This Girl is Fine!"

I respect other's opinions and compliments
Trust me that they are not ill spent
However I know without a word
From another for in my spirit is heard
The affirmation that challenges me to be
All that I am and was created to be
And I respect also the fineness in you
So to your own self let it be true

NOW
Let me share this as I conclude
My declaration of the fineness I exude
You can experience it if you have good taste
If not then I will be a total waste
And that is okay I am not for everyone

Some will appreciate and from me some will run
Some will walk with me and some stay behind
But either way I know I am some kind of fine!
Stilettoes or tennis shoes I toe the line
Of Womanhood seasoned with some kind
The world cannot miss me
Nor can it dismiss me
Opportunity cannot resist me
Nor kindness fail to kiss me
History will list me and a good man will wish me
To be his because of the fine…
That is in me

So I set to the task every day
Of being the finest in the finest way
As I am
So shall I stay
Storm and rain
Sweet breeze and shine
No matter the weather I know this better
My self is so very fine

On the Table

List the Three Major Issues that you can draw from this piece for consideration and why you consider it an issues:

1.

_____

_____

_____

_____

_____

_____

_____

2.

_____

_____

_____

_____

_____

_____

_____

3.

_____

_____

_____

_____

_____

_____

_____

Out the Door

List what you have learned and how you can communicate and implement it better on life.

1.

_____

_____

_____

_____

_____

_____

_____

2.

_____

_____

_____

_____

_____

_____

_____

3.

_____

_____

_____

_____

_____

_____

_____

SULLEN SERENADE

She sits at the table on the 33rd floor
She has broken the ceiling and controls the door
She can handle her business like any man
In fact some jump at her command
She drives the BMW and a Mercedes too
She has designer apparel with matching shoes
She stands out among women in a powerful way
Their opinion is often "well what shall I say?"
She has a way about her that will capture your eyes
Too much gaze will render you paralyzed
She is a diamond refined and she is cast
As one with a brilliance that will surely last
Her money is flowing and if you saw her house
You would exit with a falling mouth
She has it like that and please do not hate
Because most of us do not have what is on her plate
BUT
When we are not looking and she winds down
A different sort of person is down
She closes the door and flips her wig
Crawls in a space not too big
AND CRIES LIKE A BABY LEFT ALL ALONE
That would be alright if she were but she's grown
With a lot of space to feel empty in
This is her story listen to how it begins…
As she shares her heart:
"Mama told me to get my own stuff
Stand up and be strong and tough
Have a man when you want but do not need one
There will be plenty around when you are done
I took that line of taking care of your man
And it does not matter when you stand
I heard that a piece was better than none at all
And expect him to answer a few other calls
As long as he treats you right and your kids

But child I am here to pop the lid
HELL NO!
Here what I say before you go
Break this mold and do not duplicate
Anything here and live in my fate
She said get your own money and do not stop
Until you reach the very top
Owe no body and forge your own way
She said "Listen little heifer to what I say"
I love your daddy but he is a man too
Love him but know he is not you
You have to make it in a dog eat dog world
As an African American "They do not believe" girl
Kiss no ass but do not fear to kick a few
If you do not it will be done unto you
Listen to me child and you better take heed
Feed your wants but have very few needs
Buy the whole hog and sell a little bacon too
Bring some home and have someone fry it for you
Take no prisoners they cost too much to keep
Hold your own mysteries let no one peep
Your deep inner self at any time
Hear me baby girl as you toe the line
SO ~
I kissed my way to the top and kicked a few down
I shunned my mama's apron and got me a crown
I run the show and the kingdom is mine
But it sure is not what I had in mind
Talk with me sister and listen up brother
Some of this stuff was good from my mother
Pour a drink and hear what I have to say
You need to hear it in a grown woman way
You see this stuff that is around me is cool
I got it and I played by the rules
But I come in this full yet empty place
And I cannot stand to even see my own face
And I know I am finer than the average girl
I can pour on charm and rock your world
Without removing panties, bra or dress

I can draw a man's very heart out his chest
And I have and demanded he keep his pants
My response has often been "I Can't"
Because I do not want to but needed to know
If I did I could have you set on "go"
I am that kind of woman...I stand pretty tall
If I need a little somethin, somethin' all I need to do is call
And understand because I am all of this
I can get discreet and satisfying room service
But after the doing and screwing is done
After He returns to floor number one
I am laying on 1000 count sheets and a king sized bed
With nothing but emptiness flowing in my head

So...
I often pour me a drink and then take a shot
I focus on what I am and what I've got
And I feel a little better than I was
Until I come away from that initial buzz
I need to feel good and sex is not it
Something that I can snort, drink or take a hit
OF...and go where normal folk ain't allowed
Then...well...if HE came over I could again be plowed
You see when the doors close and it is just me
That corner office privilege is fake reality
I run the show and I own the floor
But life is what is on the other side of the door
YOU WANT THIS?
It comes with a damn price
Yes I could have said it better
But why must I be nice
I got a purse full of money and accounts too
And I have to be here trying to figure what to do
You would take my place without hesitation
You would not even give it examination
Because you see my fine, shine and lovers
But the funk that you miss is under my covers.
Corporate world is mine but I am stuck in this glass
I am wondering if this feeling will ever pass

Of being pimped out on my own terms and conditions
By my own self and with my exclusive permission
Have a drink sister…take some time
Hit the blunt and then do a line
Take off your shoes and walk in mine a while
Be a grown woman and get rid of your child
Where is your fulfillment and your joy?
For pleasure what tools do you employ?
Do you have it like me? Do you have it like that?
Sit where you sit that take where I have sat
Where is your child?
What has it cost you?
To do the things that you had to do…
Just to get to the top.
THE TOP!
THE TOP OF WHAT?
I look down and all I see
Is the trail of you bowing to me
Crushed heads, broken hands paved the way
Lying tongues kept me communicating what I needed to say
Shoulders broken that I stood upon much
Persons broken who formerly had the Midas touch.
That's it ladies…Game must recognize game
And whether man or woman it is all the same
Hillary is running for President and the nation is pissed
Michelle is making them mad and Barrack is being dissed
Scandal is rising and Empire is being built
Too many "think they stand tall" nigga is simply walking on stilts
Funded but not founded they try to look down
On me and try to diminish my crown
But I think not because what I have got
Situates me firmly in the "HAVES" …not the "HAVE NOTS"
But too many do not see it and give me no props
This is some "ish" that needs to stop
Have a drink and sit upon my stool
It is okay…I have defined it as cool
BROTHER
You cannot compete with me in my own
I can dominate just like I have shown

My Mama birthed me just like she did you
She taught me how to handle my daddy so she taught me you
And yet you never learned me because daddy did not tell
Because that grown woman stuff Mama hid well
But I would like a true one in your frame
But unfortunately too many of you are just too lame
Do not get me wrong I am not hating on you
Brothers do what brothers do too
You can pass on bourgeois, stuck up and snooty
But lose your mind over a Kim or J-Lo type booty
Beyonce can make you want to bow and beg
For some of that fire, tail and leg
You are corporate and you can do your thing
But it takes a choir if you want to sing
To a world in a much stronger voice
And I have some vocals that make me your best choice
To take things to a much higher level
And though you feel you are God and I am the devil
You need me to rock what you cannot begin
If you want that "For Real" entrepreneurial heaven
You could not complete Eden until I was presented
You were the true man fruit but not well fermented
Until I got into you and you into me
Remember I am your garden and your tree
Alone? He said you are not good
Dismiss and discount me...I wish that you would
But even taking my stand like my mama said
Gets little more in your head
Sit down man...tell me something good
Take a drink and a hit ...I wish you would
Did your daddy tell you much about me?
What can you handle? What do you see?
Am I your equal? Do you recognize
Me as more than vagina, breasts and thighs?
SIT DOWN NEGRO! You are not yet dismissed
Scoot over here and give me a kiss
Do you recognize a grown woman's situation?
Pause and engage in a little contemplation
What is life if it is not lived?

What does it mean to have if you have nothing to give?
What does it mean to have the best sex
If after while the only cry you have is NEXT?
What is the car the clothes and the dwelling
If the life in them is not worth the telling?
What means the appearance and the shine
If the best of me cannot be mine?
Are you listening to me…or are you a little high?
I drink the best and this is uncut cocaine
It can create fire or make it rain…
So talk to me before I lay down
Pass that quart over here of Royal Crown
Hey sister come back and sit with us
You probably have some things with me to discuss
YES YOU!
Sit down and have another drink
Into this funk with me come and sink
They do it all the time so should we
Let it be girl…just let it be
I can do what I want and so can you
But can we ever really be true
To who were are if we play this game?
Can we stand or shall we be lame?
For at the end of the day I want to feel good
As a grown woman can and should
And the stuff that is around is not more than
What I can use in my serving hand
I speak my own words
I deserve to be heard
I live as I can
And yet I cannot stand
That no matter my setting and all my getting
I am still letting…
Too many things and others control
My mind, body and soul
Getting paid
Getting dignified upper echelon laid
Penthouse cell
My beautified hell

Casket dressed
In the very best
I got it all and yet when I fall
No one picks me up from the floor; I cannot call
ANY BODY who really gives a well…
You can tell…
I am just tired of this…stuff
ENOUGH!
I am tired of drinking and drugging to forget
The emptiness from this life set
I am becoming what I am not to be as I am
And to tell you the truth "Who gives a Damn?"
If you do not and you say it is okay.
You will just live this tragic life to the fullest another day
Sit down girl have a drink and a hit
You are me get with it
Hey Brother, with us come and sit
You gave us this chair
We sleep in the same bed
This crazy thoughts and aspirations
Are infections from your head
You laugh at it
And you spit
The same lines I do while spiraling down
Trying to cope with the stuff around
YOU
That is in you
Doing what you let it do
Cause that is what you do
Awww, hell you understand
Sit down
Take a drag
Want a line?
Take a hit
Life with all the frills still ain't much
When you cannot live with yourself and touch
The deeper self just shut it down
Let silence be your sound
Just…

Have a drink or pop a few…it is all the same
Put something in this life other than the same old lame

On the Table

List the Three Major Issues that you can draw from this piece for consideration and why you consider it an issues:

1.

_____
_____
_____
_____
_____
_____
_____
_____

2.

_____
_____
_____
_____
_____
_____
_____

3.

_____
_____
_____
_____
_____
_____
_____
_____

Out the Door

List what you have learned and how you can communicate and implement it better on life.

1.

_____
_____
_____
_____
_____
_____
_____
_____

2.

_____
_____
_____
_____
_____
_____
_____
_____

3.

_____
_____
_____
_____
_____
_____
_____
_____

BEDROOMS AND BOARDROOMS

He said "I can give you this if you get with me
I can make things happen and let some things be
If you will afford me the pleasure I can do this for you
And Baby no one can beat me making it do what it do
I can give you the position and money you could never earn
You can be my assistant and live with no other concerns
Don't leave me hanging like this you know what I desire
You need to come on and catch this fire

A lot of women would jump at the chance
To get this kind of man and accept my dance
You know you want it and you want it now
I will excuse your ignorance and teach you how
To get up on loving and in your career too
What I offer to you has been offered to only a few
Holler at me now and turn down the lights
Let me show you how to treat me right

His hands were smooth and strong close to my skirt
I said "Well, a little cuddling will not hurt"
Then he became aggressive and I could feel his heat
I backed away for 10 seconds and 5 feet
He came back this time and presented evidence
That he had totally crossed the fence
And he was taking me with me without my consent
He had come and then he went...

I was naked in his eyes
I was ready to be had
And I am being truthful
Although this is bad
I was headed with him
Until he said something I hate
"Baby let me have some
Take the lock off the gate"

I calmed me down
Had to change course and mind
Ice water was in order
A chill I needed to find
I backed away from the saddle
I pulled my own reins
I composed my own self
I went against the grain

Easy now…I told the brother
I want to be close but don't need the smother
I can see some things you want from me
But slow your roll on my bra and panties
I want to be handled but handled right
I am a journey not a quick flight
There are some things you must put on my plate
If in this engagement you want me to participate

Handle your business…I know that you can
I like that and it is sexy in a man
Do your thing and make it do what it must
But let me inform you of a few thing if you want my trust
You see I like what I like and you will learn
I want what I want on equal terms
This is full fact and there is no debate
If bedroom or bedroom is to be good I must participate

Not passive…no I am not speaking of just being there
I am speaking of being equal partner with an equal share
I am speaking of getting some of what you do
I am speaking of you giving up some quality you
I am not that kind of hit it and quit it woman
I make impressions wherever I walk and I stand
Hear me now and please get this straight
If you are going to be successful in bed or board I must participate
Smooth talking and a dinner will get you a restaurant check
But it does not make you privy to anything below my neck
A movie and a dance…a night out is fine

Tell you what…you pay for your and I will for mine
If you think that will get you in my skirt or pants
Some women will but let me tell you that I can't
Let myself go that cheap and become a repository
For your body fluids and story~ that will not be my story

I cannot be climbed like a horse: ridden and whipped
Not treated as an appetizer drowned or dipped
In a sauce and consumed before the main meal arrives
I am sorry my friend…I do apologize
I have needs and I serve them because I am fully me
I am going to get mine and it is helpful for you to see
That I like standing here with you talking face to face
Saying a bedroom or boardroom will not be successful…
If WE don't participate

Now let me share some principals to help you out
I can write them down for you…there is no need to shout
I want you to be successful now do not get me wrong
But I do not want to be discounted and placed where I don't belong
I can be had but I into having too
If you want to have me you have to bring a YOU
And let me make this much clear from the start
I am not into renting, leasing or bartering my parts

I do not need your either if that is what you want to give
I need a man with whom I can really live
A man who knows what a girl like me really needs
And will wait on me hand and foot aiming to please
A man who knows that I will go beyond the call of duty
I have to give him more that breasts and a little booty
I will raise him up and make thank God above
For all the woman that He made and filled with love

You cannot rock my world if you fail to live in it
You cannot visit it or come to only spin it
You cannot be my man and ignore that I am me
You cannot treat myself like a secondary ME
You cannot run through me when you are feeling hot

And feel that I am good until you hit THAT spot
Single, married, separated divorced...get this straight
Nothing gets me if I do not fully participate
My bed is mine at least one side of it
And with no covenant baby you do not fit
When we step out and do business in the street
My principles remain as strong as they are upon the sheet
I will not work for another and be treated as low count
Equality in work and pay is what I am about
You can run the show without me but not the best
So back up and let me get these things off my chest

I will make it good
The best you ever had
I will raise your levels
To good from ultra-bad
I will make it more
Your business will elevate
But understand this now
I WILL PARTICIPATE

Participate in wages
Participate in promotion
Participate in leadership
There need not be much commotion
Participate in credit
For the stuff I truly do
Participate by standing on the stage
Visible just like you

Participate in stock options
And in the future decisions
Be all woman while standing with the big boys
There shall be no sudden or subtle division
Participate in policy making
And who stays and as well is fired
Participate so well that my participation
Keeps participating after I have retired

If you write the checks you get the pen from me
Business like sex is not about you or I but WE
I will not give it up…men or pen in bed or boardroom
And without my full participation both are doomed
But together we can make so real stuff work
More than artificial screams and sudden jerks
We can build a world grand and great
If we build it while both of us participate

I am not for humping
I am not for thumping
I am not for convenience and fun
Second class and then dumping
I am not for hiding at certain times
I am not the one to be left behind
I am not the wife silently stored
Left to the pleasures of her man and properly stored
I will cost you Baby
I will not come cheap
The stuff in and of me
Means you must come deep
To get the really good stuff
This one thing I will state
You must understand clearly
I MUST equally participate

I rolled up on him
With a hunch in my back
And an itch I wanted to see
If he was man enough to scratch
I locked myself down
I locked him all the way out
I kissed him and whispered
"Do you see what I am about?"

My man cooled his hand and suddenly stepped back
Looking like a train that had suddenly jumped track
He looked surprised and embarrassed at his pants
And said Baby you mean…WE CAN'T?

I told him that He was fine but I now could see
I could use him and he could use me
And if he had kept his mouth shut that he would have found
That I was willing with him to go a few rounds

I gave him his wallet
I gave him his pride
I gave him the opportunity
To leave and take a ride
I gave him a moment at the door
I picked his shoes up from the floor
I looked again and gave him a kiss
Backed away saying politely "You are dismissed"

Did I say he was fine?
Oh he was fine and I wanted him full throttle
But I saw that all his wine was gone
Who needed a decorative bottle?
I said "Move along and take your tired self home
What you bring to me I can see I can get alone
I laughed as he walked out my door and through my gate
Glad my eyes recognized with Him was nothing with to participate

On the Table

List the Three Major Issues that you can draw from this piece for consideration and why you consider it an issues:

1.

_____
_____
_____
_____
_____
_____
_____
_____

2.

_____
_____
_____
_____
_____
_____
_____
_____

3.

_____
_____
_____
_____
_____
_____
_____
_____

Out the Door

List what you have learned and how you can communicate and
implement it better on life.

1.

_____
_____
_____
_____
_____
_____
_____
_____

2.

_____
_____
_____
_____
_____
_____
_____
_____

3.

_____
_____
_____
_____
_____
_____
_____
_____

ONLY WOMEN BLEED

And God said "Let there be...
Until He
Me
And We
Then I heard...
BE...
Fruitful and multiply
Replenish the earth
I out of him
He into me
We
From I
And
The blood flows
I bleed...
Alone
Come to me
Enter and dwell
Share and cultivate
Place the good
And leave it to be
Stirred and situated
Come forth and into
I feed the seed
I release what meets
What is released then cage it
Feeding it
Caressing and containing
Kings and queens
Rulers on deposit
Geniuses and philosophers
World Changers
And the most subtle
Seemingly unengaged man
Who sneaks upon academia

And the most erudite
Explaining universal concepts
And eternal truths
 I bleed
I need not be cut
I am the pool
Civilization draws from
Every month I am possibility
Nile-like beyond Egypt
Fertile Crescent
Rising and falling
I am prepared
Seeking what may be
Cultivating and capturing
Prayed for
Fertile yet not always full
I wait
I am
Life giver
I am cradle and so necessary
That without me there is no other
To be called me
See without ground is seed
But not sown
Grown
Owned and replicated
Even if sown
If not held and fed
Made sick
Disproportionate when filled
Stretched
Marked and remembered
I bear then birth
Expelling what was minuscule
Thrusting into a world
Unknown
I bleed alone
Even when
In the blood of who I am

There is no life
Filling
Cramping at time
Bloated
Struggling for ¼ of a month
Irritated
I planned nothing here
This time but because I am who I am
I can be depended on
To Bleed
You see my drain
My pain
My "Oh no not again"
Popping Ibuprofen
Rocking like a baby
Cursing Eve and wondering
What it would have been like if...
Shunned during a time
I need sharing more
I Bleed...
Puberty then menopause
A long road
I bleed...
Bearing the inner and outer
I flow and carry
I birth and then the blood of me
Continues...
I feel
What is of my blood is of my being
My man flows
My children flow
My self flows...
Caught in an existential inescapable assignment
I bleed
Never ceasing
Comforting him
Birthing them
While I just...Bleed
I do not flaunt my blood

It is inside building
I release it privately
Like tears
And pain
Like sadness and disappointment
I bleed for my children living in breech
And for my man in his struggle
With dignity and impotence
Calling him forth
For he empowers me
And is me…I bleed
That he might come forth
As he did in his mother's womb
I call him
Come…dwell with me
Be of me
Remember
I am of your blood
Covering your very heart and breath
Come
No one can bear it like me
No one can help
It is heavy then lighter but IS
When nothing sown
Comes forth…
Feel my loneliness Adam
When you do not sow me
Forget me not for new streams
And fresher ones
I have given and…
Your legacy is in me
Your name is mine
I give life to you
I need your deposits
For long after childbearing years
Blood flows still to my heart
My mind
My body is full of vessels
Stimulated and delighted

Setting off things
That set you off
And fill me that you might know
The fullness of my filling
Stir my blood
Because a neglected heart bleeds
Inside OUT and then
When it overflows
I remains in places
Undesigned for it
Poisoning the vessel
That genuinely brings life
I bleed…
I cease the flow yet I do
Yet give birth
I have reproduced
What is yet flowing and will flow
I teach it
That it might continue
I bleed…
Remember that life is in me
Of me
I bleed
I am your life
Desiring your life
That we might feed what we seed
And grow forever

On the Table

List the Three Major Issues that you can draw from this piece for consideration and why you consider it an issues:

1.

_____
_____
_____
_____
_____
_____
_____
_____

2.

_____
_____
_____
_____
_____
_____
_____
_____

3.

_____
_____
_____
_____
_____
_____
_____
_____

Out the Door

List what you have learned and how you can communicate and implement it better on life.

1.

_____

_____

_____

_____

_____

_____

_____

_____

2.

_____

_____

_____

_____

_____

_____

_____

_____

3.

_____

_____

_____

_____

_____

_____

_____

_____

SUBMISSION

She began
SUBMIT!
That is what we are told
Submit!
Let the man have control
Or better yet be the head
That is what is said… to US
Respect your man
I agree
I owe it to him
Like he owes it to me
I like a man in charge
I like that masculine cover
That secures and adores me
That is labeled my "for certain lover"
I think it is what God order
No, I know it to be true
So if marriage is my thing
I do what I have to do
At least that is how I feel
I need to be cared for
I need to be WITH someone
I do not just take a name
And then my life is done
I bring something to the table
That must be recognized
So one cannot get it twisted
There will be no surprise
When I stand in my place
And present me as my own self
Not doing my man's expectation
I take me off of the shelf
To show him first who I am
The type of rib that I present

Flexible without being compromising
I am unique without his consent
And if he sees that he will be blessed
He will be able to appreciate
That in living and serving in this life
He has more than HIM on his plate
That was and is my philosophy
And I made it strong and quite clear
But the one I connected with
Obviously did not take the time to quite hear

He started well
Yes I was just right
No battle or fuss
No major fights
He expressed his take
On relationship and the make
He opened doors and walked with my hand
In his and I felt that he was a real man
His mother raised him
His daddy let him down
He was yet doing his thing
He would not let me down
Then he shared with me a beautiful ring
That made me holler and want to sing
He said he would love me till death do we part
He would give me his body, soul and heart
He would honor me and would understand when I say
To him I would love, honor and obey
Five years of heaven and then we went to hell
You will understand as this story I tell
He took over without any permission
To bring me, his wife, into total submission
Cursed one day and then threatened another
Jealousy raged and my person he smothered
His house not mine and his money too
Do what he wanted just because he wanted me to
Words got hard and he did not care
Where we were he gave not a damn or a care

I became something less that a wife to him
I wanted out for life seemed grim
Then he said if I'd leave I would regret
The repercussion I certainly would get
He took my keys and regulated my time
My mama said hold on and toe the line
I expressed my concern but she said she knew best
He was just a man handling his own business
I ask if daddy had done the same to her
She said yes but challenging him created a stir
Besides, he paid the bills and worked all day
So she let him say all that he wanted to say
It was how men were and would certainly be
So she expect the same honor out of me
I said that I would hang on and do my best
But I need to get some things off my chest
No man would cause me to bow out in life
And own me like a slave yet be called his wife
I spoke to my man to make that perfectly clear
That brother looked at me and said "My dear
You know I love you and would not say
Anything to mislead you in any sort of way
But you will listen to me like the kids will too
Or else a man has to do what a man has to do

THAT BROTHER
Raised his voice and spoke down to me
Treated me like the child...
The woman he refused to see
He said that he owned me
That I would do as he said
And if I did not
He would go upside my head
Well,
I took it as word and walked away
Did as I was doing without hesitation
He asked, "Did you hear what I say?"
I said "Nigga please!"
And I meant it just like I said

"Let me get some stuff in your head...
I aint your tramp
I am not your piece or whore
If you want to trample me
You can take it out the door
I did not marry you to be mistreated
I did not need one to put me down
And if you think that this is what you will do
The wrong woman you have found
Now let me tell you before you speak
I respect every part of you as man
You may raise your voice and a few other things
But do not ever raise your hand...
To strike because I am a black woman
And I have been raised to be strong
You can put your hands a number of places on me
With my permission but upside my head it does not belong
Hear me now Baby...
I love you to death
And for you I would even choose to die
If it were necessary but please understand
That "beat down disposition" do not try"
I thought we were cool
I thought we had an understanding
He cooled out well
I thought we had found a landing
We were doing our thing
We were making tracks
Then he got tangled up with some others
And he had a setback
He walked in the door
And got in my total space
He raised his voice then his hand
And struck me in my pace
It felt like fire
I sounded like thunder
I looked at him angrily
And I said, ": I do wonder...
If you forgot what I told you

In the very beginning?
I wonder if you recognize
I am not grinning?
I wonder if you think...
If you think I am standing hear
To submit to this degradation?
Do you think this is fear?"
He reached back once more
And I reached for my purse
Offering him a bullet and funeral
Plus a ride in a hearse"
He cowered down
He apologized
I spoke to him "too late
You need to rise"
My finger trembled
I had not settled in my mind
Whether to shoot or save him
The Negro was in a real bind
He said "You will not kill me
You do not have the balls..."
I said "You will not be able to use yours
So now you make the call
Get on your knees
Say a real prayer
Trip if you want to
I offer you this dare
You see I am tired of you threatening me
I am tired of your trips with power
I am tired of having to look over my shoulder
Now you can meet your maker this very hour"
I put that pistol in his ear
I said "If you ever try this again
I promise to run through this bullet so true
That you will understand that although you are my man
You will not do what you want to do"
He said..."I believe..."
I said, "Shut up"
I prayed with eyes open

I had to be tough
But I did not mind going to jail
He hit me in my face hard and fast
I wanted the satisfaction of just
Kicking his a _ _
Just one time
But I felt sorry for him
I loved him and I felt the anger dim
I sat on the floor and said "Baby please
Do not stand up but get on your knees"
He felt me weaken…I did too
He felt this was his chance to do
What he needed to get through
He came to my waist…"Hell no Boo!"
I thought for a moment
Then picked up the phone
I said "Pick your poison Baby
It is jail or be gone"
I said "dial the number
Yes dial 9-1-1
You are going to like this
And for me this will be fun"
He slowly dialed like he was not sure
But he knew my patience would not long endure
He said hello when the operator came on the line
I said now you will do what I say this time
OR ELSE…
I said "repeat these words in her ear
Operator I call and I do fear
That I hit my wife and made a big mistake
I need help so that in the morning I may
On this side of a beautiful grassy ground
Trace this call and here my sorry butt may be found
I abused my wife like I had no sense
When she told me that such behavior would cross her fence
Have they left yet operator? This is serious
You must stay on the line while I discuss
My trifling behavior and stupidity
Operator are you still listening to me?

This is not the first time but it will be the last
Operator please hurry them I can feel the blast
Of gunpowder and shell in my head
I can see smoke and blood
I can taste the bitter lead
She is looking crazy by I dare not say
Anything that would take her in a detrimental way
Operator…she said thank you
For sparing my life
She will end this call
And cease being my wife
There is a knock at the door
She said I have to go
Oh operator…
I love you so~"
The officer said "Mam please drop the gun"
I said I will after I am done
This man hit me with an open hand
And if after this he is released please understand
That if he ever comes back to this door
You can pick up next time bleeding on this floor
This is not a threat but a sincere pledge to do
What the system may be hesitant to do
I will not run scared nor be afraid of jail
No man will ever raise his hand to assail
Me and think that I will take it again
It is alright officers if you say AMEN!
I dropped the gun then said "I have had enough
Officer I will place my own self in cuffs
You have to do your job so I will not fight
Arrest me and then read me my rights"
The officers looked at me and said you are
So much in control why don't you drive our car?
Take him in yourself and we will come along
Stupid he is and locked up is where he belongs
My husband said "Wait…you are giving her permission
To take charge of me?
They said it is called submission!

On the Table

List the Three Major Issues that you can draw from this piece for consideration and why you consider it an issues:

1.

_____
_____
_____
_____
_____
_____
_____

2.

_____
_____
_____
_____
_____
_____
_____

3.

_____
_____
_____
_____
_____
_____
_____

Out the Door

List what you have learned and how you can communicate and implement it better on life.

1.

_____
_____
_____
_____
_____
_____
_____
_____

2.

_____
_____
_____
_____
_____
_____
_____
_____

3.

_____
_____
_____
_____
_____
_____
_____
_____

CHURCH GIRL

You see me in the place I stand
I appear as the dream of the best man
My skin is soft and my hair flows
My eyes compliment my lips and nose
I am established and gifted
I am saved, whole and sanctified
I am a godly woman obviously
I am not merely a church girl for the ride
I am strong yet tender...A living oxymoron
I am cultured, classy and my man's glory
I am not hesitant to speak what many but leak
My testimony, my history and my story

You see I am a church girl
This much I do confess
I am my Daddy's daughter
I am wonderfully blessed
I live righteously but I DO LIVE
Like one who knows what to do
Whether life is good or it is bad
I can make it over and make it through
I carry my bible and sing my song
I worship God and give him my praise
I walk with Him day to day
And the standard in me I daily raise

You look at me and you say I am out of touch
You tell me that I do not know your world
You tell me that I am caught in fantasy
Because you misunderstand what it means being a church girl
You see these diamonds and my dress
You get caught up in stuff that I wear
You think I am taking and often faking
What I am and pretending to be "There"
You think you are hard and raised in the street
But you do not know what it is to have leaves as a sheet

You think you know struggle because you have to study
Try having pimps, thieves and thugs as childhood buddies

You think you got to make it by yourself
And no one knows your hard road
But you have opportunities like never before
And you are your only load
You think the days now are harder than the previous ones
You think the world owes you for what you must live
You think that God is wrong because of the song
That you have chosen and feel you must give

You think my praise is not authentic enough
You think I come to church for mere fun
You think I am born out of ease and privilege
You think I am here until I haul tail and run
Because life gets real and I get scared
Because I feel the weight of the world on my shoulders
You think I am sharing and not really caring
About real life now that I am older
You think I do not know pain, disappointment and struggle
You think that if I encounter it my head goes in the sand
You think you know more but let's take the floor
Let me show you what I understand

You see I was not born in the church or in a palace
I was born into what was a bad situation
I was not born of love nor much other you could think of
That would make you want to live in my station
Mama was Mama but she was not right
My Daddy was a man of mad temper and rage
The got together and in passionate engagement
Scripted my life upon the page
I came here and hard was the arrival to be
I found nothing very welcoming to and for me
I found a place and lived in a space
That just let me be what I would let me be

Fights and shouting became the music in my ear

My vision was filled with "not good"
I learned to cope with the liquor and dope
I thought it was normal though not understood
I heard the cursing and felt the fear
I adjusted to the vile expressions and threats
I took what I could and kept it tucked away
No one must know it was in my hand
I became a survivor as out of necessity
Of myself I made obsessive demands

Because life was cruel and although Mama cared
I was not what a child should be allowed to be
She had her own way but I did not stay
Where I could live and play safely
Sometimes we would smile and have a good time
Sometimes all hell would flood our home
Sometimes I clicked my heels to get that "Dorothy Feel"
Wishing I could leave rather than go home
I knew of God and that when we went to church
We were to meet him for worship and prayer
But I could not relate to Him on this date
I felt that obviously he could not care
For...

If He did I could live better than this
He would kill the man that caused Mama Hurt
He would give us more than the crumbs of life
He would have people treat us as more than dirt
GOD CARED?
For others maybe so
But in my life that statement earned a "NO"
I may have sounded irreverent
But I was what I felt in my heart
And from that disposition
I promised to never part

Then my dad pulled a gun and gave a shout
He pointed it at my mother's head
He promised to kill her and it chilled her

Until a police officer shot his trifling self dead
He bled and died and soon was buried
I loved him but was glad he was gone
It is sad to say but this was the only way
He was ever going to leave us alone
NOW WHAT do we do?
Now how do we make it?
I was a teenager now
I could barely take it

I was flushing out and looking fine
I was sexy without having to try
I could catch a man without laying a hand
Upon him and only feeding his eye

I found them cruel too but usable
You had to know what you were not selling
You had to keep what was best to yourself
And keep your deepest riches from welling
They were buying and I made some offers
I learned to get by and along
I learned to forget and yet
I knew this was not where I belong
I despised myself and this weak crowd
That I felt that I had to navigate within
I did not want to stay in this nefarious way
I wanted this to cease…I wanted it to end

But Mama said you are never broke
If you have one of these between your legs
Work it well and keep it free from smell
And for it a thousand dollars will beg
She said you can rule a world and any man
Take a lesson from my "Get it Girl" playbook
Feed him until you establish your own will
Get him well out the water and deep on your hook
And I knew she was right but the cost was high
I also knew that I could learn to pay it
The game was hers to win and when she was in

All others rose, bowed or would sit

She was my adolescence and my example
She taught me more than anyone else
She made me strong although also wrong
She taught me how to live on and off the shelf
She told me to leave the religion stuff alone
She told me conscience and guilt were but lies
That no one could nudge me nor could judge me
But God and what I saw of myself in my own eyes
She told me to tell others to kiss my behind
She told me to look out for myself alone
To use you like you would use me
And when you left to let your tired self be gone

She got in sister and you look at me
Like I do not understand what it is like
To live in the world because I am a church girl
Oh ~ you really do not know my fight
A man wanted to locked me down
A lover who wanted to take my stuff
A would be pimp walked away with a limp
When I said "Hell, I have had enough"
Making it on pennies rather than dollars
When I decided I wanted to go straight
Lying and crying because there was no money for buying
And all of my bills were terribly late
Children were had with men who did not care
Who acted like the father I had known in earlier years
But I let them pass and did so fast
I could not bear to cry my mother's tears

I bore the scorn of people looking down on me
I bore with the shame and the accusations
Of being a loose woman and of low class
I was treated like a true abomination
Marked with scarlet symbols and letters
I was the one with all the bastard children
Others were issued warnings about who I was

And to hold very tight to their men
I knew them alone and prayed for a well
That maybe I could talk to a good man at
Without him filling it his duty to get some booty
Because what he saw on me was PHAT

Church….?
Please?
God?
You must be kidding!
I have seen them when I was a child
And God still did not know my house
I would not go because this I did know
He did not understand what I would talk about
I got the saints out my face with bibles and all
I told them to be affectionate where the sun don't shine
Heaven was not real and hell was what I had most to deal
I told them to find someone else upon whom they could grind

My world fell apart even more than before
My kids grew up and gladly ran out the door
Loving me and yet desiring to be free
I saw in them what I wished I could be
I was working my game but I was tired now
Their leaving allowed to better operate
But I was caught in a fix and this was it
I could survive but did not want this fate
The world I was in was so artificial
Yet that was where so many dwelled
Talking about keeping it 100% real
But they were actually incarcerated in self-made cells

Mama as hanging by a thread
Daddy was so thankfully dead
Siblings were trying to get and out
Of the mess and pain we knew so well about
Children were running from labels and past
Boyfriends were still boys and not men that could last
Girlfriends were hanging like me in tight places

Dolled and laughing wearing masks as faces
Bitter and wanting to throw a middle finger to the world
Are you listening to the emergence of THIS church girl
You think this is an act and I am out of touch
This is only a little said here of what is so much

Sit yourself down and take your pen out
I am praising God with a hand and a shout
Because after all the denial I put Him through
He came to me and only then I grew
I got up from a place I had grown to love
That had the base person seemed to be above
Where I was and who I had become
I felt last to all and never number one
I am the Jezebel washed and Gomer redeemed
I am the Rahab on the block and Mary with the cream
I am the woman with the issue of blood in a crowd
I and the one made to cry "UNCLEAN" aloud

I am the one good enough to talk to in the shadows
But never good enough to go to Mama
I am the one caught in the middle of so much little
The one always participating in all of the drama
I am THAT ONE who walked down the aisle
To the whispers of others saying "Not that one child"
I am the one that no one wanted to sit next to
I am the one who was often sitting on the back pew
But it was okay because He was with me
It was okay because I was free
And I did not know anyone else's story
But I saw no halos over them or inherent glory

Sanctified
He set me free
From all the fingerprints upon me
Justified
I could now live large
Before Him for there was no charge
Glorified

I was more than I seemed
My God hold me in high esteem
Adopted
The enemies plan was thwarted
I am now my Father's daughter
Reconciled
He took all my stuff off the shelf
And got me back to Him and in touch with myself
Secure
Out of the shadow of a life so dim
I have an eternal place in Him

I saw the folks at church
An the ones that were truly saved
Some just passed by me
And at some I paused and waved
But I knew who I was
And I knew who they were too
But I came to God for my own self
And to Him I would be true
I liked me
And I like plenty others
It felt good in my world
To know new sisters and brothers

Hypocrites? Yes some of them were
But that were plenty of them in my world
What was in the street I knew I would meet
In the sanctuary as a church girl
So I sucked it up and I rode with God
And I never chose to look back
I did not try to persuade all the minds that were made
To think of me as they did I just changed tracks
I took my steps and I see you
Thinking you can do it alone too
I do not sweat it because I get it
I have done all that you seek to do
But let me say this so that you will know
You think what you think but it is not true

You are the fake one trying to live a life
Far from God and what was never intended
For you or any other well-meaning woman
Your heart, mind and soul must be mended

You can run as you will and do your own thing
You can hustle and hang like he matters none to you
But you will discover as did I and my mother
That to Him one day you shall be accountable to
Tell the world to go to hell
Use all the folks you desire to get to the top
Discount the rules and use the tools
Run over what you will and refuse to stop
You can do it yourself and keep it too
You can be everything you want in your eye
But one day you and your stuff shall fade away
You will lie down naked and broke to die

And there will be no world for you to enter
You will be homeless in eternity
You will be undressed and in a mess
Then what I am saying will become reality
But it will be too late and no one will be there
To listen to you nor help you again
You chose your world and well...
Hell awaits you and that is your end
HELL?
You do not believe
Well that is a choice
Its goods you shall receive

And hey...It's not for me to argue with you
Do what a world girl has to do
I have been there and I know what it is like
'I know the script
I know the fight
Rock it, drop it and walk it too
Whip it and make it twirl
But to him I give my heart and soul

To me He is the Lord of my world
So go on and for you and so shall I do
Loving myself as a church girl

On the Table

List the Three Major Issues that you can draw from this piece for consideration and why you consider it an issues:

1.

_____

_____

_____

_____

_____

_____

_____

2.

_____

_____

_____

_____

_____

_____

_____

3.

_____

_____

_____

_____

_____

_____

_____

Out the Door

List what you have learned and how you can communicate and implement it better on life.

1.

_____

_____

_____

_____

_____

_____

_____

_____

2.

_____

_____

_____

_____

_____

_____

_____

_____

3.

_____

_____

_____

_____

_____

_____

_____

_____

INSIDE MY MIND COMING AND GOING

I am me
In case you want to know
I am not struggling with saying
What I want you to know
At times
And it causes others to think
That maybe I am not here
But there is a link
Between what I say
And who I can show you
I hope you can understand
What I am going through
Before you judge me
Understand my case
Know what I tell you to know
Shut up!
Hear me speak in my place
You see
Age plus health
Time plus wear
Have cost me some wealth
And some partial tears
My mind is strong
But it also is tired
It is loaded with knowledge
But sometimes it misfires
And others think that I am gone
The think I am absent
The think I do not belong
In the places I have been before
They look strange in my face
Thinking I am not safe
I need another safe place
But I know me
I talk with myself every day
I get my own thoughts out
I hear what I have to say

And if you cannot hear me
You need to listen more closely
You need to learn to comprehend
The language of me
I hear others saying
She cannot do it alone
They speak of my options
Like I have ears of stone
And cannot hear what is being said
Like I am heavily discounted
And two steps from being dead
They want me comfortable
The want me safe and secure
They want me out of the way
And they want to be sure
That no harm comes to me
And I truly understand
But I am yet independent
I am still my own woman
I may not be as strong as I was
But I can handle my own business
I can move assuredly beyond
Speculations and a good guess
When...
I remember what it is I am to do
For sometimes on my way to this
THAT is what comes through
And I get it done
In a backward kind of way
I can figure it out
And I understand what they say
Tomorrow confuses today
And tomorrow has not happened yet
Day before yesterday confuses
Weeks coming and I fret
These thoughts will not stay in place
In fact I sincerely doubt
That they will and then
My loved ones will surely find out

And...
The discussion begins again
Maybe of assisted living
But they are not considering
And assisted giving
Come and go as I please
That is what they have said
But is that really true
Or something they want in my head?
But they can kiss my behind
They can hit the door
They can go wherever they want
I do not need them any more
I can cook my own meals
I can clean my own house
I can run my own errands
I just need help getting about
I can...well...maybe not by myself
What need I to do?
What must come off my shelf?
We were talking about...
Well, you know what it was
It is your time to speak
This ever increasing fuss
Has me confused for a moment
Let me sit down
Let me get on one channel
I do not need all these sounds
That echo in me
When I want to be alone
Do not tell my children
They will want me gone
Among all those old people
Who are not able to be
Eight plus and able to discuss
What it means to be like me
Capable of doing your own thing
Driving and hanging tough
But the agenda I admit is quite a bit

Consuming and also tough
But I am not going down
I am not going in
I am standing strong
And I will defend
My rights to live free
My own place is mine
My money is too
I can do me
Just like you can do you
Except
I am scared
Because I do recognize
The confusion in my mind
And before my eyes
But I do not want to be cast out
I do not want to pushed
I will not submit the rest of my life
To a gerontology ambush
Do not see me as crippled
I do not need the nurse
I want to communicate with you
Do not make me curse
Because I will if you keep saying
This same crazy stuff
I appreciate the concern
But enough is enough
I wish I could trust you and...
You crew as well as cronies
Some of you are alright
But a hell of a lot are phony
Counting the dimes
Weighing the benefits
Of putting me away
Of putting me on the night shift
And they do not see how aware
I am when they are speaking
Information is flowing
And truths are leaking

I want to get help
But not lose control
Of my own life and living
I know that I am old
But do not underestimate me
Do not underrate me
Do not understate me
Do not mistake me...
For an incompetent...
I want your help
But I am not invalid
Do you understand?
I want to be me
With a little help
From you...by you
I can be transparent
With you
If you
Will keep it between us
And not hold it over me
If not...leave me alone
Let me be
Whatever I will be
On my given day
Let me live part-time on my own
And otherwise step on
Because I will live my life as grown
Until growing stops and I am in the ground
Then and only then...
Will I not share my own sound
Do you hear me?

On the Table

List the Three Major Issues that you can draw from this piece for consideration and why you consider it an issues:

1.

_____
_____
_____
_____
_____
_____
_____
_____

2.

_____
_____
_____
_____
_____
_____
_____
_____

3.

_____
_____
_____
_____
_____
_____
_____
_____

Out the Door

List what you have learned and how you can communicate and implement it better on life.

1.

_____
_____
_____
_____
_____
_____
_____
_____

2.

_____
_____
_____
_____
_____
_____
_____
_____

3.

_____
_____
_____
_____
_____
_____
_____
_____

THE DEVIL'S SHADOW

You will find that your memory falls short
When faced with this affliction of the evil sort

The betrayal of your own reflection avails
It is a story that in time of itself will tell

You obviously do not know your rightful place
Your heart is blackened and ugliness is upon your face

You may forget the people that your evilness has touched
But we will not forget, as the magnitude is much

Your treachery has gone beyond that of a fool
Instead of using love for good, it is used as the devils tool

But eyes are open and you're seen from miles away
So the Christ within me goes to bent knees to pray

Your inheritance is due and collection is a must
On that you can depend and in it you can trust

I will pray for you to go and go far away in deed
For of your bitterness, I truly have no need

Go to the dark where the moss and fungus grow
That's where your evilness is born… in the devils shadow

On the Table

List the Three Major Issues that you can draw from this piece for consideration and why you consider it an issues:

1.

_____

_____

_____

_____

_____

_____

_____

_____

2.

_____

_____

_____

_____

_____

_____

_____

_____

3.

_____

_____

_____

_____

_____

_____

_____

_____

Out the Door

List what you have learned and how you can communicate and implement it better on life.

1.

_____
_____
_____
_____
_____
_____
_____
_____

2.

_____
_____
_____
_____
_____
_____
_____
_____

3.

_____
_____
_____
_____
_____
_____
_____
_____

COLOR MINE BLACK

I feel the eyes looking hard at me
Wondering what is on my mind
Some sincere and some in fear
Some want to kick my behind
Some think I am unique
Some think I am in a phase that won't last
Some want to stop and talk
Some want to walk past
Some wish I would be who they say
Some value how I'm different too
Some think I am faking my funk
So say..."Do what you do"
Some won't see my beauty
They are stuck on my skin
Some think that is where
The deeper woman begins
But if they would look beyond they might know
The treasure of any person or thing
Lies in what is below....
THE SURFACE
Can I be me?
Can I have my desire?
Can I like what I like?
Your smoke is not my fire
Can I change who I am?
Can I choose and pick?
Of who and what I want
This is not some kind of gimmick
I am not insensitive to you
But I need to be real clear
That this is me and how I live my life
I am not caged in doubt or fear
I love and respect you all
Do not get me wrong
I live my own music

I write my own song
My vanilla color is what you see
But you are unfamiliar with my flavor
Your presumption causes you confusion
When you discover what I savor
You have problems and think I betray
My people because of this fact
My preference in who I desire to be with
Is not what you thought...it is Black
Do not get me wrong I am not blind
I am not confused in my head
How it shall be, but I am saying for me
I desire from a chocolate vessel to be fed
You look harshly at me sister
You are embarrassed because of my parents too
But look you do what you want
And I say "Bravo" to you
You may desire Exxon as your gas
You may shop at Walmart of Kroger
You may buy your clothes at Belk's
Books from Amazon, Kindle or Dover
But that does not mean that they are for me
I can get the same thing from another place
What I like is outside of my ethnicity
It is not outside of what is our race
For it is human
No matter the cover
I desire a man
Who would be my lover
A man of character
A man of God and style
A man committed to loving
This Vanilla Child
Who has a desire for who I am within
Who hungers for who I am
Who sees beneath my cover HIS desired lover
And to others does not give a damn
Sister you say I am taking your man
Because he is Black

I should stay within my own color
And let him come back
But I do not seek to take him from you
I am a great man's choice
Of the darker skinned persuasion
And when I hear the voice
Of God say "You are his
I made you for his life
As his needed rib
Assume position as his wife"
I will go forward
I will receive what He gives
I will love him like no one else can
For as long as he lives
He will be mine
That is no slap to you
He will be a great man who's Black
And is MY dream and Boo
And to you my parents
Who say I was not raised
To be with another not as I
Do not be amazed
When I tell you I have been
What you raised me to be
My own real person
Grounded, perceptive and free
I love you dearly
But please understand
You will not disrupt the thing
I have with my OWN man
You closed the door
You told me to choose
Between a man I love
And you and what I lose
By continuing to prefer him
And go against your will
I choose ME mom and dad
I have a destiny to fulfill
Perhaps you do not get it

Perhaps you do not want to
What I want is for me
It is not for you
You have in you what you were born with
And you passed that on to me at birth
Black was not what I was made for
But you like purple and did it occur to you
It is also a mixed composition of color
Drive a red car and truck too
Ride Union Railway or Amtrak
A vehicle or a brand is what it is no matter the label
As a loving man is who happens to be black
And to you my brother from another mother
The preference in my style and make
Let me be clear so I do not steer
You into error or call it a mistake
I love your shade and your culture too
I love your genetic and spiritual contour
But with open eyes seeking no surprise
I want the deeper inner man for sure
I seek not your body because of infatuation
I'm way beyond the lies and the myths
I seek who you are and know you're raising the bar
Because I am THAT kind of woman to be with
When you see me peek inside my soul

And then you can put my container in view
You cannot like what you have to fight
But if I am her then something may be here for you
But if not them keep on stepping
There is nothing here for you in my walking
I need no one who is finished or done
Because has game but makes no sense when talking
And let me say this to you dear mister
A woman of another ethnicity is my sister
You cannot use who I am by further trying to disrespect her
And use me to say that you need a white girl
Because I will do anything to get in your world
She is who I am in spirit, body and mind,

And know I shall and will kick your behind
She is a kindred soul and I pay attention
To how you treat her and Oh ~ did I mention
I can get what you have easily if you are no extension
Of something greater than you...I desire another dimension
Holler at your girl
See my integration
Vanilla chocolate composition
In both quite a sensation
Your sister, child, lover and friend
As neither do I lack
What it takes to be great in them
Just because my preference in a man is Black

On the Table

List the Three Major Issues that you can draw from this piece for consideration and why you consider it an issues:

1.

_____
_____
_____
_____
_____
_____
_____
_____

2.

_____
_____
_____
_____
_____
_____
_____
_____

3.

_____
_____
_____
_____
_____
_____
_____
_____

Out the Door

List what you have learned and how you can communicate and implement it better on life.

1.

_____
_____
_____
_____
_____
_____
_____

2.

_____
_____
_____
_____
_____
_____
_____

3.

_____
_____
_____
_____
_____
_____
_____

OFF THE STAGE

The clock expires
The day ends
The curtains fall
I take off the mask
I take off the costume
In the privacy of a quiet
Backstage dressing room
Lights are down
No more applause
I must relieve myself
To live a nobler cause
I play many roles
And they come to an end
When they do
A new episode begins
I do what I do
To get what I need
But that you must understand
Is not my real speed
You see there are parts of me
That simply must perform
They match in certain phases of life
But are not what I truly adorn
What I truly am is written
By me on my own book page
But there are other chapters of me
That are from my life on the stage
Do not get carried away
I have a stage name
But I and who that is
Are not the same
Do not misinterpret the line I read
The words are for me and the part
But that is given for me to say

That is not the ME of my heart
GENERAL POPULATION
THAT ME that you see
Smiling all the time
Taking crap from everyone
Pretending it is all fine
Is not who I am always
Do not make the mistake
Of thinking you can bring more B.S.
Because I have a large capacity to take...
Oh you will be surprised
You will be amazed...
It is not like that sweetheart
When I leave the stage
I can be the DIVA
I can be the best friend
The enduring employee
Who never gets to ascend
When we are playing
When the show is up
But I will be your monkey
Holding the change cup
I have seen it too often
I have played the role
I have danced to rhythm less music
I have acted warm when cold
I have bowed to the lesser
Because that was the dialogue on the page
Until the show was over...
And I left the stage
NOW
Let me get it straight
Let me make this clear
Open your eyes
Clean your ears
There is a side of me
Comprehended only with my permission
Do not define me too soon
Do not mistake my submission...

TO your opinions and view
To your rumors and lies
To your presumptions of me
You see I wear a disguise
Because thieves break in
When they think you are not at home
But the me you think you may know
Has never let you in her home
MY BROTHER
Who thought you saw me dance
All seductively that you had a chance
You thought the sweat of my breast and on my face
The fun of the exercise of the floor with him
Might just give him a warm place
Between my legs and upon my breasts
After a few drinks at the after party and some rest
I saw you looking deliciously at my behind
And felt you trying to take a little in a dance grind
You were rolling to and I liked your moves
You and I were attractive and worked real smooth
It worked with you and it was not surprising
That in both of us a true temperature was rising
You were loaded and packing as if taking a long trip
I never heard you say it but I could see it upon your lips
You thought the smile and the passion in me
Could be his because he was fine as hell and sexy
He wined and dined me like a Casanova charmer
But I also saw in him and undercover farmer
Who already had a tractor but needed a hoe
Who thought that mine was the way to go
And he wanted to plow me if I would allow
But to this encouragement I would surely not bow
I sent him back to his seat after I turned the page
Read the last page and left the stage
He cried "What did I do? What do you mean?"
I said "Last act Baby…end of the scene
You wrote yourself a part as a leading man
But you need to get this and understand…
I do what I do because I want to

And it is obvious I could do you if I wanted to
But I needed some fun; I needed out of MY own cage
Now I am going back to it...I am leaving the stage
MY SISTER
Hollered at me and spilled her heart
She needed to vent and I played the part
Of the one who would listen because it was right
I understand when a woman is having a fight
I sympathized and opened my door
Cried with her and walked the floor
So she could work it out and feel better again
I got to that point and that is when...
She started showing up and showing out
She thought my life was hers that she had clout
My stuff was hers and I was hers to command
I got no requests just repeated demands
She believed I was taking it in but she was mistaken
She found herself in her own cesspool and was shaken
She asked me what happened and if she had been played?
I said, "No my friend...I have just left the stage
I do what I do for you as you asked of me
A friend in need was all I was meant to be
You took control or at least that is what you thought
But I am not to be controlled by one ticket you bought
You have to understand that I do not trust so fast
And after I helped you get on my feet you looked past
Who I was and what was on my personal agenda
You forget I was brown sugar and not fake sweet like Splenda
I read you and let you audition for me
And that is when it became clear for me to see
That I do not need friends like you to feed my rage
So turn the lights of when you leave for I am leaving the stage
MY BOSS
Oh how I hate the word
But since it is what it is
I will let it be heard
I run your show
Only when I am there
But the rest of my life

Don't you dare
Seek to control by pay or hour
I work and live on my own power
I determine the path
I determine the grade
That I will live on
While I work your stage
No in case you missed it
Or even got it twisted
THIS IS NOT IT
I soon will diss it
Because I want to
I will be my own loss
Of your guardianship
I will be my own boss
I will give you my best
I will make you shine
I will be responsible
I will toe the line
I will make it happen
For you at the bottom of your page
They will applaud you for me
Upon your own stage
But even while on yours
I play my role
And awards go to many
That give you the hold
That you want therefore know this
If you really like that wage
You better treat me right
While I am on your stage
AM I THREATENING YOU?
No…This is mere sound advice
Person to person communication
Advising you to do me right
Holler at your girl now
You will be later be amazed
At how much you will need and miss me
When I exit your stage

MY CHILD

I am your mother and gave you birth
I see your potential and your worth
I see your true self and I am proud
That you will obtain all that is allowed
But your days of raising are over
You must stand on your own
I want you to know what it is to be grown
Wash your clothes baby with your own dollar
Dry them too and you do not need to bother
With bringing them to me to do them for you
Your mother has some other things to do
Buy your toiletries and watch your spending
No more overcompensations from me...it is all ending
Which means you pay back as in a loan
And if you do not then lending privilege be gone
What's that you say?
I owe you much more?
You are asking me "What am I tripping for?
Let me be candid with you baby...let me be sage
I case you did not know...I have left the stage
Now do not get me wrong I will care for you
But not like you have been accustomed to
For you must move on and I must also
We just have different places to go
You thought I could not endure the empty nest
But I assure you Baby that Mama knows best
I provided for you from birth to college
But let me impart to you some new knowledge
You are now going to stand here with me
I am going to show you what you will come to be
I will show you what to expect that comes with age
I am no longer Mama Provider by Mama Mentor off stage
18 years was plenty to get you to know the role
To grasp the storyline and the message being told
4 more years to help you get on your feet
Note I said "Help" perhaps this message I should Tweet
So you will understand how life truly flows
How people are seen, appreciated and chose

I want you to know Baby that the previous phase
Has me now exiting and you entering my stage
Assume the position and watch your turns
Watch your expressions and from me learn
That you must now master the adult craft
I am not your cruise line now just a needed raft
Pay the bills baby and make the choice
They will pay you to sing in your own voice
Wait the tables and be willing to do the long hours
Of study and sacrifice that bring you true power
My debt is paid and now I wean you from me
Always attached but you need to truly be free
And you cannot do that on my dollar and dime
I will be right in front of you and you are still mine
But Mama has to do woman now and to her end
I will always be your mother and now can be friend
MY SELF
We have made some trips
We have sacrificed a lot
We have been the "have"
We have endured the "have not"
We have made things happened
We have seen some things die
But self I must say
I have enjoyed you and I
Now we enter a new era
One that gives is the chance
To meet the prince
And enjoy the dance
We have the years to take the gaze
Write a new life headline
And make the front page
Fabulous woman walks the runway
And leaves the world silenced
Not knowing what to say
We will give them our pen
We will make it real clear
We will communicate what they need to hear...
You are fine and you know it

You are fertile and you need to grow it
You are awesome and you need to show it
You have a horn and you need to blow it
Come off the shelf and take the stride
Take life with you on a serious ride
Open to me and give me revelation
Defy your norms and your expectation
Rise up and walk like you always desired
Feed your passions and your fires
You can walk the jungle and parried; come out the cage
A new life has begun on another stage
Swing in the black dress and stilettoes
Let destiny take you where it wants you to go
Write that new chapter on all of those pages
Live victoriously on all of your desired stages

On the Table

List the Three Major Issues that you can draw from this piece for consideration and why you consider it an issues:

1.

_____
_____
_____
_____
_____
_____
_____
_____

2.

_____
_____
_____
_____
_____
_____
_____
_____

3.

_____
_____
_____
_____
_____
_____
_____
_____

Out the Door

List what you have learned and how you can communicate and implement it better on life.

1.

_____
_____
_____
_____
_____
_____
_____
_____

2.

_____
_____
_____
_____
_____
_____
_____
_____

3.

_____
_____
_____
_____
_____
_____
_____
_____

WHAT A GIRL WOULDN'T MIND

A girl wouldn't mind
If a man takes a look
At what her as a woman
And was appreciatively hooked
He may look one time
Well, maybe more than too
As long as she feels respected
When the looking is through

A girl wouldn't mind
If a gentleman would say
"I am really interested in you"
In a gentlemanly way
She would not mind an invitation
To desert or coffee
A little conversation perhaps
Something just might be…

A girl wouldn't mind a conversation
About a book read and enjoyed
She wouldn't mind a man of class
And certainly one who is employed
A girl wouldn't mind getting to know
A man who would like to know her
And then get to know as he will show
Significant things in his taste
And what type of woman he really prefers

A girl wouldn't mind a little wining and dining
She could us a night or two on the town
She would not mind giving because it is part of living
Some things also to make the relationship sound
A girl would not mind some quality attention
She would enjoy a little affection

She could enjoy and relate the progressive date
As long as it headed in the right direction

A girl wouldn't mind being a wife
If the right man wanted to be her husband
She would gladly share and lovingly care
For the one who would want to be her man
She would love him to death with each breath
She would capture him and allow him to find
All of her treasure and true wealth in her without measure
She really would ~ A girl would not mind

A girl wouldn't mind being a full-time lady
She would not mind being a lover
If she is loved in return she would learn
To balance that with being a mother
A girl would not mind setting off
Alarms walking her personal runway
She would not mind a man at work
And certainly not one at play

A girl wouldn't mind just being a girl
It is what a girl is supposed to want to do
And if you observe you will want her to serve
A bit of her good world to you
A girl is a lady, a woman and blessing
Oh ~ so many other roles in her you can find
If you enter the right door, she will let you explore
What is in her ~ a girl really wouldn't mind

On the Table

List the Three Major Issues that you can draw from this piece for consideration and why you consider it an issues:

1.

_____

_____

_____

_____

_____

_____

_____

2.

_____

_____

_____

_____

_____

_____

_____

3.

_____

_____

_____

_____

_____

_____

_____

Out the Door

List what you have learned and how you can communicate and
implement it better on life.

1.

_____
_____
_____
_____
_____
_____
_____
_____

2.

_____
_____
_____
_____
_____
_____
_____
_____

3.

_____
_____
_____
_____
_____
_____
_____
_____

SPICEE WOMAN PLEDGE

I will recognize the wonder of my womanhood and celebrate it every day.

I will recognize the royalty of my lineage and carry myself as a true queen.

I will honor my God as designer and sustainer of who I am and make known to others that I am no ordinary person.

I will honor the legacy of my ancestors and understand the importance of sustaining that legacy.

I will recognize my ability to grow and develop things and will use that skill in my everyday life and business affairs.

I will be whole within myself before I ever seek to be whole with anyone else.

I will avoid unfruitful relationships that strip me of my dignity and self-esteem and will only engage in what makes me and that person better.

I will give myself to the man whom I believe God gives to me and who will see me as a necessity and not an option.

I will honor my man as my king in my life and reign with him as one in our personal kingdom.

I will raise my children in a spirit of excellence and purpose never allowing them to settle for mediocrity in their thoughts and pursuits. I will become intellectually excellent, economically efficient and ethically exemplary.

I will never compromise my dignity and character for an advantage.

I am too valuable to be discounted, too wealthy to be treated cheaply and too powerful to be handled in weakness.
I will take my place in the world and make it better by doing what I do best. I am not common or ordinary by any means for I am a true SPICEE WOMAN.

SISTER TO SISTER WITH NO MISTER

Personally
Please understand
I love me some males
But I do not need a man
I am all woman
I am fine to the bone
I love myself
I do not feel alone
I am not strange
I am not queer
I just prefer me a woman
When I need someone near
I am not unlike you
I am still your sister
I just prefer for myself
A Miss not a mister

I love smooth like butter
I love so very much
Another woman's understanding
Another woman's touch
I love one like me
Who understands my personal need
Who is kindred in ability and desire
And is willing to nurture and feed
Back up from looking funny
You are not so always drawn to men
It is not because they are not fine
It is not because you cannot blend
But there are just some times
When you relate better with a girl
And a man is a total disruption
If he enters your world

Now this is something I need to say
Something needs to get in your head
This is not about getting laid
It is not about sex and bed
It is not about what you are feeling
It is not what gender we are screwing
It is about one sister with another
It is about what we like doing
I am one of you
I need you not to ostracize
Who I am though a lesbian
I need you to be recognized
I am not after your daughter
I am not after you
I just want to be a sister
Doing what sisters do

I am still a lady
I still have a sister heart
I still am not angry or bitter
Let's get this straight from the start
I like to get my nails done
I like massages and pedicures
I love shoes and clothes
Fashion enhancement is a cure
When I need a lift
When I want to be pampered
You see being a real lesbian
Does not cause these to be hampered
I do not wear a label
That says "I am out of the closet"
I will not shame or de-fame you
You need not fret
Hear me for what it is worth
I will not hide this in a whisper
I love me a good man
But I want the love of a sister

I can rock my dress

The pants I can wear
I can turn heads for many reasons
In just about anywhere
I can run with the big boys
I can stand as a true lady
I can represent true womanhood
I need not be false or shady
You would love to be like me
For in all I well represent
Who you would want your daughter to be
Besides my sexual preference
So why don't we cut that out
You are entitled to disagree
On this point and keep it moving
Just let a sister be

I can run the government
I can roar on the stage
I can get a rise out your man
If my skirt is raised
I can run the show
I can educate
I can make your point and mine
I can win the debate
I can fight on the field
I can be the one in command
I can be in authority
And still honor the man
I can take a blow
A wound, hurt or blister
And still be a lady
With no desire for a Mister

I am not your fire
I shall not try to ignite it
And you are not mine
I do not have to fight it
But you do not really know
What turns me off or on

Other than what you think
And that thought needs to be gone
Work with me ladies
Please get this
Are you drawn to the total male
Or is it just the penis?
Is it not the whole man
That you should really desire?
I am just asking
I thought I would inquire

So do not think all is want
Lies between another woman's thighs
I want more than sweat and breasts
More than sexual highs
I want more than what is before you
I want more than what is behind ya
I want a total woman whole in package
I want much more than vagina
I do not want to do the male
I like who I am
This is my confession
I do not give a damn
I just want a few moments
To talk sister to sister
I am one just like you
I just do not want a Mister

And to the brother who is looking
Saying "What a real waste"
You like what I like
You understand my taste
I have heard in my ear
These very things being said
Many men have the fantasy
Of two women in the bed
Do you think it's all for you
When a woman cooperates?
When one is doing you like you want

She is being served ~that's no debate
She is not being ignored
She is not waiting her turn
She is not being untouched
There are things she will learn
You are considered normal
You're just getting you some tail
Instigating two sisters mixing par time
While you get on your male
You call me a bull dagger
You call me a dyke
But if I never spoke intimately to you
All about me you would desire and like
I am like your mother
I am like your girl fantasy
I am like the boss who runs the business
I am truth and reality
I am like your grandmother and aunt
I am like your dear sister
I just have my own preference
And it is not for a mister

God loves me too
That much I know
Because the same bible you read
It tells me so
He does not condemn me
I am not going to hell
No matter what you say
THAT is a hard sell
Until I see something different
I shall not budge
So why don't we just get along
Who are you to judge?
I will not interfere with what you believe
I will no call you homophobic
Because you do the heterosexual thing
I will not call you sick

AGAIN

Accept me for who I am
Yet live in your own world
I am just asking for you acceptance
As full person and full girl
I like who you are
This world is for us
To learn and understand
To honestly be open and discuss
Who we are and what we like
What we do and what we don't
Where we go and what we stay away from
Where we will and where we won't
Holler at me when you want to
I am still your warm blooded sister
Just like you both loyal and true
I just prefer one like ME not a Mister

On the Table

List the Three Major Issues that you can draw from this piece for
consideration and why you consider it an issues:

1.

_____
_____
_____
_____
_____
_____
_____
_____

2.

_____
_____
_____
_____
_____
_____
_____
_____

3.

_____
_____
_____
_____
_____
_____
_____
_____

Out the Door

List what you have learned and how you can communicate and implement it better on life.

1.

_____
_____
_____
_____
_____
_____
_____
_____

2.

_____
_____
_____
_____
_____
_____
_____
_____

3.

_____
_____
_____
_____
_____
_____
_____
_____

I WILL LOVE THE REST OF YOU

The diagnosis was not good
She cried as it was thought she would
They said it was cancer of her breast
A mastectomy was needed and best

She cried and said "I do not think so"
I will be less woman if this goes
I cannot be the woman he needs
This much I can already concede

A few years ago you said to me
I had to have a hysterectomy
You took from me my womanhood
You said I should have understood

I am struggling with menopause
And you add more issues to my cause
You are taking me apart part by part
I am so much less than I was from the start

NO! She said, and walked out the door
I came to be healed…I need to be more
I am going to another for another view
I am not going to let you do what you want do

She went to her husband and she cried
The tears flowed powerfully from her eyes
She said "they want to take all of me
I want to be a woman and the cannot see

I want to love my woman like a whole woman
Because you still are the best of man
I want to be my very best
They want to take from me my breast

They want to take even more of me
Baby I just cannot let that be
My hair will fall out and I will be sick I cannot do
this...It is a trick

They just want my money
I think I am healed
I cannot do it my love
This is a bad deal"

She fell down into his lap
And he held her while she took a nap
He stroked her hair and told the physicians
I will speak to my love so she can listen

He prayed for her and she heard his voice
He whispered, baby let me help you with this choice
I love you just the way you are
You are my sun, you are my star

I love your whole not just your parts
To lose you would simply break my heart
The breast they say will soon kill you
I am not will to lose you for you to keep two

Anything that hurts you cannot remain
To me that is the ultimate pain
I want you in my arms and when they are through
I will love the rest of you

Give up the hair for a short season
It will be for a very good reason
I will shave mine ~ that I will do
And I will love the rest of you
If you are sick for a while I will share

On the Table

List the Three Major Issues that you can draw from this piece for consideration and why you consider it an issues:

1.

_____
_____
_____
_____
_____
_____
_____
_____

2.

_____
_____
_____
_____
_____
_____
_____
_____

3.

_____
_____
_____
_____
_____
_____
_____
_____

Out the Door

List what you have learned and how you can communicate and implement it better on life.

1.

_____
_____
_____
_____
_____
_____
_____
_____

2.

_____
_____
_____
_____
_____
_____
_____
_____

3.

_____
_____
_____
_____
_____
_____
_____
_____

AND SO THEY SAY....

My hands, they are worn
And my heart has been torn.
My eyes filled with tears
For things heard by my ears.

My breasts sit no longer
High upon my chest.
I do not feel as though
I am as worthy as the rest.

My hips are a bit hipper
And my thighs are a bit thicker.
And my ass, my sweet, sweet ass,
Has become close friends with the grass....

My legs once lean and strong,
Now their strength seems to be gone.
A young woman I say I am
And they look at me and shake their heads
..... Umm, umm, umm!

You're too young to be so old.
You're too warm to be so cold.
The say youngster, raise your head up high,
Take a deep breath and stretch towards the sky!

Look around you, and then look inside.
Live the truth, never live out a lie.
You are a woman, beautiful and strong
I say I am used; they say I am wrong!

I say I am hurt and my hearts filled with pain.
They say that I am blessed for all the knowledge
That I've gained.

I ask what good is that when I feel as I do.

They say the choices are mine, they say it's all up to you.
I say I don't understand why my life must be this rough.
They say ain't life a bitch girlfriend, tell me, ain't it tough?

I ask why? Why must this be?
Why can't he see what's inside of me?
Why must I struggle to pay bill after bill,
What must I do when I lose my will?

They ask; do you not have a roof over head?
When you sleep at night, are you in a warm bed?
When your tummy is hungry, do you fill it with pie?
You know there are some so hungry that they literally die.

I feel bad for them; really I do;
 But that does not stop me from feeling so blue.
I say that I'm fat and feel undesirable.
They say that I am giving and that that is admirable

They ask what brought me here to this state that I'm in.
I say I really don't know where my life began to sin.
I say I've fallen down hard and simply lost my grace
And that I just can't keep up with this erratically set pace.

I say my pride is all but gone
And that my back is no longer strong.
My determination has been shattered
And my heart is broken and battered.

I do not like the way that I live
I try so hard to love and to give.
They say destruction is never the way;
Live for tomorrow, live for today!

Lift your head up child, raise it high
Look every man straight in his eye.
Love only one that's wholly yours,
But love yourself ever so much more.

Smile every morning that you awake;
This life for granted...child do not take.
You are a woman, black and blue.
You are my sister, tried and true.

You are a woman, a "Giver of Life"!!!
You are a woman who should live without strife.
They say that I am wonderful, exceptional even great,
They say that my spirit he simply cannot break.

They say that my soul is sensational and unique,
They say that my mind has never been weak.
They say that my heart is in the right place
They see it in my eyes
They see it on my face

.....and so they say.

On the Table

List the Three Major Issues that you can draw from this piece for consideration and why you consider it an issues:

1.

_____
_____
_____
_____
_____
_____
_____

2.

_____
_____
_____
_____
_____
_____
_____

3.

_____
_____
_____
_____
_____
_____
_____

Out the Door

List what you have learned and how you can communicate and implement it better on life.

1.

_____
_____
_____
_____
_____
_____
_____
_____

2.

_____
_____
_____
_____
_____
_____
_____
_____

3.

_____
_____
_____
_____
_____
_____
_____
_____

EMERGENCE

He made her…
Out of
Connected and inseparable
If he was to have her
Covered by him
Yet not inferior
Where did the idea come of…
Him being superior?
Pushed back in time
In purpose and power
It was her day… It was
her hour

Dissatisfied
She was awakened
She was disturbed
She was shaken
Strength suppressed
Equality denied
Her existence was devalued
She would no longer take this ride
She was told to stay in her place
She was told to stand down
And be glad to have a man with her
She was told "keep your feet on the ground"

Her man was her ruler
He son would soon pass
Her in stature in the home
Into a much more elite class
"Have the babies
Make the bed
Lay when I need to lady
That is enough said!"
She was told what to do
She had learned where to go

Until she woke up collectively one day

And just said "HELL NO!"

Out of the shadows she came
To the forefront
Ill-regarded Black
Insufficient white
Red rejected
Asian ignored
Minority misrepresented
Disqualified by estrogen
Trampled by testosterone vials
Labeled to be kept
For future reference But not used...

She was desired
But not thought to be wired
To be what a man was
Therefore she was placed
And replaced
For she did not see her place
In the space she was relegated to
Therefore she moved
And the needs and wants
Of the men who came there
Were not met
Because they had moved

She emerged tall
Raising standards and hands
Dignified defiant
Demanding to be counted
Refusing to be invisible
When she saw herself as she did

Speaking in a voice
That demanded to be heard
Not because it was loud

But because it had something to say and the rest of
humanity of which she was a part would listen....

She maintained her home
But was large enough to occupy more
She stood at a window
And walked out a door
She seemed to he man
To live in sedition
Rebellion of a new sort
She was no longer bound by tradition
She was showing up off the chain
She was beyond the field
She was using her own voice
Not yielding it solely to masculine will

She took her place in the world
It had been taken
Designated
To where she could not be seen
She redefined it
She owned it
Pulled it to an equal place
At the table of dealing
She spoke as a partner
God gave both dominion
She challenged the status quo
With rich thought and opinion
She has marched in the street
She went to the ballot box
She made them open to her
What heretofore had been locked

She has run for the office
She has won many chairs
She has made her true mark
She is climbing the stairs

She still has the challenges

But she still is willing
To make strides for her daughters
As they crack the glass ceiling
She has arrived and is still coming
She is crossing lands and waters
Awakening the consciousness
Of not only her locality
But her global sisters and daughters

She is the glory and honor
Of every truly good man
And she must be recognized
If the human race is to stand
She is the blessing emerging
She is doing her thing
She has a "solo" component
Yet with the choir of all can sing
She makes it all better
Wherever she goes

On the Table

List the Three Major Issues that you can draw from this piece for consideration and why you consider it an issues:

1.

_____
_____
_____
_____
_____
_____
_____
_____

2.

_____
_____
_____
_____
_____
_____
_____
_____

3.

_____
_____
_____
_____
_____
_____
_____
_____

Out the Door

List what you have learned and how you can communicate and
implement it better on life.

1.

_____
_____
_____
_____
_____
_____
_____
_____

2.

_____
_____
_____
_____
_____
_____
_____
_____

3.

_____
_____
_____
_____
_____
_____
_____
_____

SO I MOVE ON

Here we are in this awful place
Saving goodbye; trying to save face
Because what has happened did not need to
It was a decision and an act that you chose to do
You told me that you did not want me any more
You showed your backend then walked out the door
You thought I would pursue you but I just stood still
My heart said "go" but my mind said "chill"
You do not want someone that does not want you
Remember that over is over and through is through
So I let you go and take your chance in the street
And resolved the demands you made I could not meet
AND
I found the courage to face family and friends
Who ached to find reasons that brought about our end
I put up wedding albums and pictures we had taken
The emotions were too powerful; I was too shaken
THEN
I cursed you inside but I never said a word
"To hell with you" was the echo that was heard
In my spirit and I meant it when I said it then
I regretted every moment you ever touched my skin
I tried to pretend that you really did not matter
But then how could I explain how I became shattered
If I dismissed you as the source
It's awful the way that things came to an end
Oh ~ how I longed for you to feel my pain
Not only as a visitor; I wanted it to reign
In your life and kick you as brutally as you kicked me
And make you feel my despair and total misery
THEN I SAID
Wait a minute ~ this is my life to live
And although you are gone I still have a lot to give
I was your blessing and you have made me your loss
But I am still in charge of me ~ *I AM MY OWN BOSS!*
I will not fail to live because I have been kicked aside

I will brush myself off and I will rise
Out of my ashes, my misery and despair
I will see a new vision and breathe some fresh air
AND
I will thank you for whatever I can
Give you back your ring and take back my hand
And it will not take you long to realize
That you picked the wrong door and forfeited the prize
You will discover what you became was not you alone
You cannot be who I helped you to be when I am gone
SO
I have no regrets and I will gladly sign the bill
It is your choice darling ~ it is your will
I am a whole person now although I stand alone
I will make a fresh start, farewell, be gone
No need to remain where the thrill is none
Let the doorknob hit you where the Lord split you
AND NOW I MOVE ON!

On the Table

List the Three Major Issues that you can draw from this piece for consideration and why you consider it an issues:

1.

_____

_____

_____

_____

_____

_____

_____

_____

2.

_____

_____

_____

_____

_____

_____

_____

3.

_____

_____

_____

_____

_____

_____

_____

_____

Out the Door

List what you have learned and how you can communicate and implement it better on life.

1.

_____
_____
_____
_____
_____
_____
_____

2.

_____
_____
_____
_____
_____
_____
_____

3.

_____
_____
_____
_____
_____
_____
_____

WHEN WILL IT BE SAFE?

When will it be safe for me to let my guard down and trust that you will guard all that I am simply because you know the treasures that I hold within?

Will I be able to cry without it being perceived as a ploy to use my femininity to assault your masculinity? May I cry simply because my tears are cleansing and I am washing away hurt that has accumulated in my heart? I do not want to give these negatives light in order for them to develop into an unattractive picture that you could essentially view as the true me.

Will I ever be as safe as that little girl who hides behind the legs of her Papa? She knows that the only other place that is safer than the fortress of his legs is to be held behind the gates of his arms.

Is it safe for me to enter into turbulent waters that churn and swirl; preparing to engulf and drag me into a watery descent when all I want is to be spewed onto the shore of you. A place where I may rest and rejuvenate myself before I dive back into the waters of life? There I can be assured and comforted knowing that I can always return to the safety of you.

I wonder if you will protect me from ever having my heart broken again. Is my tender heart safe from your temper, your past hurts and your disappointments? Will you shield the sensitive part of my womanliness? Its fragility lies in your hands and is seeking refuge. Will you yield to your aggressions and obsessions and vent upon the one that adores you? Am I safe from these transgressions of your heart?

When will I be able to say with certainty that he loves me and there not be an invisible question mark that lingers in the air at the end of my declaration? Am I safe and secure in the love that you pose? Is it safe for me to say with all my heart and being that I love you so much that I would hand you my life because I know with all certainty that you will guard it and keep me safe... even if necessary from you?

I need to feel safe in the knowledge that you are my guardian, my protector, my shield, my armor, the defender of all that encroaches upon my happiness. I want to feel secure in your loving embrace. So, I ask again, when... when will I be safe?

Answer:
The moment he knows that he truly loves me, he will do any and everything to protect all that makes me unique and desirable to him.

He shall give to me the haven of "him" and in return, I will give him everything good that I am with all the love encompassed in my being. Then and only then will I believe that I shall finally be safe.

On the Table

List the Three Major Issues that you can draw from this piece for consideration and why you consider it an issues:

1.

_____
_____
_____
_____
_____
_____
_____
_____

2.

_____
_____
_____
_____
_____
_____
_____
_____

3.

_____
_____
_____
_____
_____
_____
_____
_____

Out the Door

List what you have learned and how you can communicate and implement it better on life.

1.

_____
_____
_____
_____
_____
_____
_____

2.

_____
_____
_____
_____
_____
_____
_____

3.

_____
_____
_____
_____
_____
_____
_____

SO INTO ME

Life has had its share of ups and downs
Its delightful days, melancholy moments and frowns
I have had those days when I thought all was well
And those nights that seemed that I lived in hell
But that is part of living and I do not despair Life can be
hard but it is oh~ so fair

One of the things that has challenged me
Is what I have embraced when I wanted "We"
I have had images of that very special one
Only to discover that they were wrong after the fun
And the newness wore off and we stood alone
I found that person present but love was gone

I blamed myself and looked for all of my flaws
My eyes watered as fountains and all that I saw
Was a person exposed and left alone again
I knew I had to stop…yet I was afraid to begin
To see "Myself" in a whole station on my way back to me
Not wanting to live as "I" when I wanted "we"

It was important to get to know the person call "I"
I was necessary to give relationship with me a try
So I did and discovered that I am a person extraordinaire
That I am so much and that I have so much to share
 I had wasted it on those who have chosen to go
And ignored a special person in me wanting to say "Hello"

So I dusted myself off and I changed my perspective of me
Focused on myself and put off my thoughts of being "We"
I celebrated and took care of my special beautiful self
I took all of those things that I had hid off the shelf
I cared for, worked on and enriched what God created I saw
the most awesome person and I became elated

I ridded myself of the thoughts in my mind

That had caused me to become so incredibly blind
To the essence of who I was and who I could be
Sacrificing *that* person while looking for *that* "WE"
I re-thought myself, me and all that I had become
Moved up in my personal rankings to be number one

I recovered from me hurt and what I thought had been killed
God took and he handled with care, now I am healed
I ridded myself of the bitterness and that awful pain
Now I am ready to begin Again…
But
Do not mistaken what I am trying to say
I am ready to begin in a much different way

I am positioning myself for what is good for me
I am taking no resumes' for another broken "we"
I am looking for more than the color and dressing
I am interested in that one that does not mind blessing
A person who wants to be a blessing to someone too
And wants to have an ongoing love through and through

Next time I need that one who wants to be into me
Not just around me when there is extra time to be
That person who needs the gaze from my eyes
That yearns for my touch and soul deep sighs
Who has a voice and presentation that is exclusively mine
That knows my presence in soul all of the time

Who recognizes I am that covering that personal fashion
Reservoir of service, friendship and inexhaustible passion
That wants all of me and desires to bring out my best
That will give me not just something but that hidden "Rest"
I am not interested in one who keeps me from being lonely
The love that I want must be really into me

I want one who can put up with my little quirks
Who loves me when things do not quite seem to work
I want the one who will forgive me when I have done wrong
Who will not punish me or hold anger against me for long

I desire a love I can reveal myself to and that wants to see
Only what is visible by one who truly wants to be into me

Adam was created first and then God went so gently inside
Of Adam and brought unimaginable true love to his side
And held her right there until that man could discover
That she was a gift un-releasable until he wanted to love her
Until he wanted to give all he was, sacrifice "I" for "We"
And be that one like I yearn for who will be into me

Until then I will enjoy myself as a whole human being
I will get to know myself better and keep on right on seeing
That person God so wonderfully and dynamically created
I will make sure I am loved by myself and well celebrated
I will present myself to my God and for the world to see

ME AS I AM

And if by chance life should seek to change my I into a we
I will make no changes unless I know and I see
That special one God gives who happily chooses
To bless, need and forever desire
To lovingly be into me

On the Table

List the Three Major Issues that you can draw from this piece for
consideration and why you consider it an issues:

1.

_____
_____
_____
_____
_____
_____
_____

2.

_____
_____
_____
_____
_____
_____
_____

3.

_____
_____
_____
_____
_____
_____
_____

Out the Door

List what you have learned and how you can communicate and implement it better on life.

1.

_____
_____
_____
_____
_____
_____
_____
_____

2.

_____
_____
_____
_____
_____
_____
_____
_____

3.

_____
_____
_____
_____
_____
_____
_____
_____

A TRUE STORY OF GIVING

She sat in the corner alone
Tears flowing
Hiccups
Jerking
Her heart bled in sync
With the tears that fell
She isolated herself
Fearing that anyone she see
And know her pain

It hurt
She had to be a woman
Strong
"Damn the pain!!!!!!!!!!!!
And although they see me cry
She thought
They will know I am strong
No one better bother me!
It's my business!

She was known well
Definitely capable of doing
And being what she would
No one crossed her
No one went past the door
She had erected
BUT
One friend
Who loved her
More than she ever knew
Entered her space
Quietly
Without interference

She asked him

"Why are you here?
What do you want?
I am okay!
Don't you have something to do?
I will all when I need you
Go home
Why don't you listen?
You are so stubborn!
Can't you see I don't want to be bothered?"
Shhhh, "he said
You talk too much
I am not bothering you
I have not spoken
But as I sit here
I feel you
Your hurt
Your sadness
Your isolation
Your aloneness
Your disappointment
Your grief
I want to feel it
I am your friend
I love you
You cannot handle this alone"

She said, "I do not want to hurt you
You mean too much to me"
He spoke, "When you hurt you
I hurt...I feel you
Your tears keep company with my eyes
And the flow together
That when the storm is over
They might rejoice together
Do not ask me to leave
I will not go while you hurt
While you sit in this corner
Away from me
Do you believe that I will let sorrow have you?

I love you!
I will not let pain overwhelm you
And leave at ease"
She said, "There is nothing
No one that can heal this
It is too much...
If I had...
Well, I had someone who..."
He slowly began t empty his pockets
They were filled...
Cash in abundance
Credit cards
Checks received
He laid them at her feet
She said I do not need your money
It is too much to give
Then he took off his shirt
His pants
His socks
She said this is not a moment for sex
He told her...I know but I give you myself
My whole self
Not merely of myself
But me
TAKE ME
WHATEVER YOU WANT
NEED
TAKE ME"
She cried
But...
He told her...
"If what I have
Who I am
Who you are
Will not fix this
Then I will stay here
UNTIL GOD COMES
To give you what no one else can

I will stay with you
In your situation…
Okay?
Why? You may ask…
I love you
And all I have
All I am
Is never too much to give
To help you make it"
She settled in his bare chest
Rested upon his lap
Oh my…Soft firm thighs
She felt her pain subside
Her he was kissing her tears
Her disappointment was departing
Her aloneness had found company
He took it…

She began to speak…
Shhhh, he said
Let me feel what you are going through
She lay upon him for hours in sweet repose
Losing her anguish to his reception
Resting
In his love

The dawn broke
She rose
Smiling
Thanking him for what he offered
He rose with her
She said "I love you"
He said, "I love you too…
And anything I can do
Anything I can be for my baby
Please let me know"
He reached to grab his pants
She drew near to him
Lightly pressing against him she spoke,

"You said I could have anything?
You were willing to be anything
And I could have whatever I want?"
Slowly he replied…Y E S ~
Well, why don't you give me the rest of the clothes you have left?
And baby I think I can help myself the rest of the way

He smiled, "Will I help you feel better then?"
She said…well ~
Let me put it this way…
You will not only help me feel better
You will help me be better ~ c'mon now
You promised ~

On the Table

List the Three Major Issues that you can draw from this piece for consideration and why you consider it an issues:

1.

_____

_____

_____

_____

_____

_____

_____

_____

2.

_____

_____

_____

_____

_____

_____

_____

_____

3.

_____

_____

_____

_____

_____

_____

_____

_____

Out the Door

List what you have learned and how you can communicate and
implement it better on life.

1.

_____
_____
_____
_____
_____
_____
_____
_____

2.

_____
_____
_____
_____
_____
_____
_____
_____

3.

_____
_____
_____
_____
_____
_____
_____
_____

LET LOVE FLOW:
THE BEGINNING OF A LOVE STORY

Never did he intend
Even in his wildest dreams
To fall for her as he did
He was built to be alone
Never opening a closed heart again
Love was good but too much work
An unnecessary burden
Good to have if you like pain
And have some sense of adventure
And he did not

Life had been hard for him
Relationships were fickle
Women were plenteous
Ladies were few
Sex was all you could stand
Love was scarce
Players on the field
With no true management
The meat market was opened
You could smell the taint

So he walked away
No problem
So he thought...
THEN
She came along
Brilliant as an evening star
As quiet as a gentle breeze
Moving through the trees unnoticed
But never unfelt
What? Surely not!!!!

Her vision beckoned him
"Move from where you are
Get a better view
Look deeply
You have never seen her before"
He resisted...
"NO!
Dammit self...
I told you we are not looking any more
Why must you be so defiant?

We have been here before…
Fine and intelligent
Professional and set
Driving, stylish, own home
Kids gone and on their own
Money and lonely
PLEASE!
SHUT UP SELF! I DO NOT WANT TO HEAR IT!"
He walked away
Right into her line of view

She was forward but not rude
She knew coy very well
And her voice was inviting
She knew how to use it
"Excuse me sir"
He turned to her
She called his name
Extended her hand
Looked him in the eye
And he invited that SHUT DOWN VOICE to speak

He was having problems
She was beautiful but much more
She had his attention
She asked to drink a cup of coffee with him
Just one
He obliged

She had a lot in common with that cup
Warm, sweet, tall, well prepared...
He was caught
She knew it...

But she let him run the line
He tired of evasion
She recognized his weariness
She spoke...
"Acquaint yourself with me
Tell me of you
Just a little…
24 ounces goes fast
So make my time worth it
Please..."

His heart seemed to fail
His resistance was gone
She asked and he gave
WUSS!
Where was his manhood?
He was buckling and she was getting what she wanted
And she was polite about it
Non-intrusive
He fell slowly into her presence
With no exit strategy

If she was not so kind
So beautiful
So polite and compelling
He would call the police and have her arrested
He felt totally violated
For he was naked before her
With his own permission
No secrets!
And those he had kept he was now telling
Without force or persuasion

What kind of predicament was he in…?

Then he said…No need to fight. So he did not
He settled into her and they talked
She seemed to know what was open in him
And what was closed she did not disturb
He did not mind….he thought!
Or did he?
What was it about her?
He enjoyed her company
A man can change!
She wound to the end of her cup
The last ounces…

She drank them and he felt they were soft
Entering the sweetness of her mouth
He watched as she took them in and touched her lips with her tongue
Right when he was about to share with her
She grabbed her purse and rose from the table
Beauty and elegance stood in her shoes
This was no ordinary woman
She was special
He offered to purchase another coffee
She said, "A true lady must be about her word

My coffee is through and therefore my time
But I thank you for yours"
He said …but I did not tell you of me
I had barely started and you are leaving"
She said, "Invite me to a moment with you
For you…We will base it on your cup
Drink slowly and we may have a little more time
Until then…thank you handsome
Be good and I promise to see you soon"
Then she walked away…

She walked and he called to her…
"Wait!
She turned to address his concern
I did not get a number for you"
She said to him…

"If you discover yours
You will know mine…"
He knew this was different
She was different
He would be forever changed!

On the Table

List the Three Major Issues that you can draw from this piece for consideration and why you consider it an issues:

1.

_____

_____

_____

_____

_____

_____

_____

_____

2.

_____

_____

_____

_____

_____

_____

_____

_____

3.

_____

_____

_____

_____

_____

_____

_____

_____

Out the Door

List what you have learned and how you can communicate and implement it better on life.

1.

_____

_____

_____

_____

_____

_____

_____

_____

2.

_____

_____

_____

_____

_____

_____

_____

3.

_____

_____

_____

_____

_____

_____

_____

HE SAID ~ SHE SAID

(Lovers Dictation)

This piece was inspired by true conversation between lovers.

He Said: You are so beautiful; that is my targeted statement for your very existence.

She Said: Well, if you keep up all of this sweet talk darling', you will receive no resistance. You are going to be loved to the extreme and I hope that you are ready for it.

He said: I will go to the edge with you all the time and know that I've prepared for every bit.

She Said: Baby... I am loving you without boundaries, do you understand?

He Said: I want to be there with you and you alone and bless you as your man.

She Said: All of my doors are open to you, this you really should know.

He Said: Whatever door you open to me, it is there that I shall go.

She Said: My well runs deep and of me, there is just so very much.

He Said: I will reach wherever you need and every area that needs to be touched. I have the key and will unlock you at will and I will know all your windows & doors.

She Said: You are one dangerous locksmith I must admit and have unlocked me forevermore. I love that there is no pretense with us, no need to even be coy.

He Said: I've conceded that you are my God given love and the destiny of my joy. You do not intrude, you do not violate, yet you invade my daily dreams.
She Said: I cannot resist the invitation to court when I am made to feel like The Queen.

He Said: I am targeting you and I want you to feel me, do you hear me "little girl"?

She Said: (While giggling incessantly) I understand and am prepared to give you the world.

He Said: I love how you handle me; my weaknesses don't scare you because here you choose to remain.

She Said: I love that you allow me access to you as this draw is driving me insane. To you I belong, you have written upon my heart and have shielded me from sorrow.

He Said: I want you to be joyful because, you make life so grand; and give hope for a brighter tomorrow.

She Said: You have an ability to take me there and then … you make me want to stay.

He Said: You will know romance and love so pure and I will ensure this every day.

She Said: There is something on my mind and I must confess I don't know what else to do.

He Said: I embrace you as you are, you may speak freely, and I am terribly blessed by you. Speak your mind and heart, do not fear; there is no judgment to be passed.

She Said: I am that good kind of bad that you speak of at times and I fear it is going to last.

He Said: Well bless your soul; I can live with that and the sweet good bad that you are.

She Said: Please know my love, you insight me to flames that could burn in the night like a star.
He Said: Beautiful, we have grown incredibly over time and you have me sweetly stirred.

She Said: My Love you strummed my heart strings and found a tune that makes me sing like a bird.

He Said: It is passion declared when a man no longer wants to start a fire.

She Said: There is no need for flames since the passion itself is fueled by pure desire.

He Said: I would rather churn in the heat of your flames; so ultimately my dear you are to blame.

On the Table

List the Three Major Issues that you can draw from this piece for consideration and why you consider it an issues:

1.

_____
_____
_____
_____
_____
_____
_____
_____

2.

_____
_____
_____
_____
_____
_____
_____
_____

3.

_____
_____
_____
_____
_____
_____
_____
_____

Out the Door

List what you have learned and how you can communicate and implement it better on life.

1.

_____
_____
_____
_____
_____
_____
_____
_____

2.

_____
_____
_____
_____
_____
_____
_____
_____

3.

_____
_____
_____
_____
_____
_____
_____
_____

TO BE OR NOT TO BE
(Letter to My Aborted Child)

Dear Lord,

I have some issues that need clearing
And
A soul that needs mending
The tear is mine
But
The only real healing must be yours

How do I begin?
How can I clear my conscience?
How can I ask my baby
A precious gift from you
To forgive me for what I've done?
I ended a pregnancy
Why?
Convenience!
Convenience?
Not ready?
Who will care?
Can't I do what I want with my own body?
These questions haunt me
My heart hurts
My arms ache
My mind is troubled
I treated so harshly
My precious baby
Innocent
Tender
So small
So dependent
Helpless

They said you were not human
You could not feel
You were not visible
Stem cells
Random chromosomes
A DNA cocktail
And
I agreed
I knew better
I can't place all the blame on them
I made the choice
I tried to calm my conscience

I said no to God
And
I conspired
With physicians and
My companion
Took my position
On a cloudy day
In a cold office
In the presence of
Poison
And instruments of destruction
Yielded myself
And
Legally
Slew my child
And faced
No charges
No one knew
No one hurt
Except *YOU*
The one could not defend himself
And now
I realize that although I left
Recovered
I am not healed

My hurt was my fault
But you did not deserve
That kind of pain
I gave you no chance
And
Now you're gone…
My precious child
Please forgive me
I know that God has a fondness for children
And although I said no to Him
About you
I know Him NOW
I wish that I did then!
I know that
He received you
What I did was wrong
You didn't deserve it
Mama was wrong baby
And I am so sorry
I have missed so much
I missed seeing your face
I missed your smile
I missed your laughter
I missed your love
I missed your friendship
I have missed all of the blessings
That your birth would have brought
I long for you every day
My tears flow constantly
And no apology makes it better
No reason explains it
I must live with it
And
Without you
But somewhere
In your tiny heart
Can you find room to forgive me?
Can you try to understand
What I meant not what I did?

OH---can you just find a space
To love
Someone who committed life's worst offence
Against life itself
Against you
Baby
This is mommy

Lord?
Will you forgive me?
Will you tell my baby that I love him?
Will you help me heal?
Will you help me forgive myself?
Because right now
I don't feel very good about myself
Will you let my baby see
Me
One day?
And will you
Let me see him
And hold him
Just one time
And call him my baby
And hear him say
Mama?

You said yes to his birth
I said no!
Will you please say yes!
To this request
And
My darling baby
Please don't say no!
I'll love you forever
And pray to see you
In eternity
Forever,

Mommy

On the Table

List the Three Major Issues that you can draw from this piece for
consideration and why you consider it an issues:

1.

_____
_____
_____
_____
_____
_____
_____

2.

_____
_____
_____
_____
_____
_____
_____

3.

_____
_____
_____
_____
_____
_____
_____
_____

Out the Door

List what you have learned and how you can communicate and implement it better on life.

1.

_____
_____
_____
_____
_____
_____
_____
_____

2.

_____
_____
_____
_____
_____
_____
_____
_____

3.

_____
_____
_____
_____
_____
_____
_____
_____

AN ALMOST TRAGIC LOVE STORY

She rose, turned to him and smiled
He walked right past her and said not a word
He went to the phone and 10 digits he dialed
And his bright communication was heard
So
She thought that she would try again
She fixed his breakfast and prepared a love letter
And although he was able he passed by the table
And said, "I like the food at the job better"
But
She smiled any way and grabbed his coat
She moistened her lips and cleared her throat
To kiss him and tell him how she loved him so
But he took his coat, raised his hand and said, "I've got to go"
Then
She saw him drive down the block and pick up his co-workers
He took time to greet them, "good morning mam or sir"
She saw that he had a totally different demeanor
She figured that he was so busy he couldn't have seen her
So
She fixed a special lunch and at noon time
She met him at work with it and looking fine
She fixed what she knew that he would enjoy
He said, "Thanks but no thanks; I'm eating with the boys"
Slowly
She left alone with her head hung down
She struggled to smile but refused to frown
And resolved that she would try yet again
Because she was his woman and he was her man
Then
She lit a fire and let the soft music play

She sent the children to family and all visitors on their way
She poured a glass of wine and ran for him some hot bath water
She put on that last special dress that he had bought her
And
She met him with a smile when he came through the door
He asked her what she had done this for
He had things to do that he had brought from work
He did not have time tonight for her; "Hope your feelings are not hurt"
However
The phone rang and it was one of his childhood friends
They talked, laughed and reminisced ~ seemed they would never end
While she poured out the wine, put up the food, and let out the bath
water
And took off the last dress that he had bought her
Desperately
She walked past him but he never turned his head
She lay down loaded with love unshared upon their bed
Suddenly she saw him emerge into their room, she got on track
To express herself to him until he gave her his back
Still
She scooted close to him and held him tight
He said, "Go to sleep girl ~ we won't have this tonight
It is late, I am tired and you want to play
I work and I have had a very hard day
Therefore
She gathered herself and rolled far enough away
That he could not hear what her mind had to say
And when the last tear was shed from his rejection and scorning
The agenda was set to be gone before morning
And
The clock rang and he felt no warm tender hand
He saw no one blocking his way when he went to stand
The bed was empty and there was no smile
He realized that this was not the morning style
There was no breakfast and no love letter

He realized that his life had not gotten better
He listened attentively for a ringing phone
He came to realize that he was alone
That he had sent away what he thought little of
He had embraced everything but the one who loved
The very ground he walked on and wanted to share
Every moment with him; she just wanted to care
And he prayed, "Dear Lord, please let her return
This valuable lesson I have learned:
Do not take for granted the love that is yours
Do not treat like trash what few can ever afford
And the Lord said, "I have these words to say
You not I drove her away
And if you would desire to have her home again
You will have to go find her and tell her my friend
How precious, how dear and how much you realize
That she is your gift from the One beyond the skies
And that you have been foolish in so many ways
And you yearn for her to return to you and stay
If you do not do that then your dearest wife
Will become your ex and the jewel in someone else's life"
He knelt down and cried and then he wrote a letter
Expressing his love for her and when he felt better
He cancelled the day, the week and vowed to suspend his life
Until he could live it only with that jewel he would cherish...his wife
He walked out the door and there she was in the yard
He said, "Hello baby, life has been kind of hard
Since you left me and I came to realize
How much you are to me; Darling look in my eyes
I am so sorry and I love you so...
Please stay with me and I will not let you go
I will love you and I do want you to love me
Anything else we can just let be
Here's my heart, my soul, my breath my hand"
She said, "I am your lady"

He said, "I am your man"

She said, "Can I relive with you the day before?"

He said, "Come on in darling; you can have that day and more."

On the Table

List the Three Major Issues that you can draw from this piece for consideration and why you consider it an issues:

1.

_____
_____
_____
_____
_____
_____
_____
_____

2.

_____
_____
_____
_____
_____
_____
_____
_____

3.

_____
_____
_____
_____
_____
_____
_____
_____

Out the Door

List what you have learned and how you can communicate and implement it better on life.

1.

_____
_____
_____
_____
_____
_____
_____
_____

2.

_____
_____
_____
_____
_____
_____
_____
_____

3.

_____
_____
_____
_____
_____
_____
_____
_____

A TRIBUTE TO MAYA ANGELOU

PHENOMENAL STILL
(A tribute to Maya Angelou)

They said you passed
That she moved on
You had taken flight
But she is gone
And it is true
I know the story is real
But even after the last breath
Maya's you are phenomenal still

Classic black
Unlike any other
You stood proud in your ethnicity
Yet you transcended color
Words danced on your pages
Sending both warmth and chills
And nothing ever shall change
You are phenomenal still

I want to be sad
But you would tell me to smile
You would open your arms wide
And speak to me as your child
You would make me understand
That life is spent working the field
All will be called in one day
But you can be phenomenal still

Farewell my friend
Thank you for the times
I have spent in your words and verses
In your rhythms and rhymes
You will live on forever
And with you I shall make this deal
Every time I speak of you I shall declare you
Phenomenal Still

THE AUTHORS

Crystal Pringle

V. Darrell Lloyd

Geneva Baker-Cotton

Other Spice-See Resources

Spice-See Dialogues

Spice-See Leader Edition

Spice-See Dialogues: Issues Edition

Spice-See Leader Edition

Spice-See Dialogues: Skits

Spice-See Leader Edition

Spice-See CD: Dialogues Volume I

Made in the USA
Middletown, DE
10 August 2015